DECORATING
PORCHES
AND DECKS

DECORATING
PORCHES
AND DECKS

Stylish Projects
for the Outdoor Room

LARK BOOKS
A Division of Sterling Publishing Co., Inc.
New York

SUZANNE J. E. TOURTILLOTT

CHRIS BRYANT
art director

EVAN BRACKEN
photography

ORRIN LUNDGREN
illustrations

———

VERONIKA ALICE GUNTER
assitant editor

EMMA JONES
ROPER CLELAND
interns

Acknowledgments

We want to say a grateful thank you
to the many people who helped make
this book so much fun to work on:
Ned Gibson at B.B. Barnes; Olav and
Glen Seimer; Bill and Judi Ayers at
the Wright Inn & Carriage House;
Lisa and Rice Yordy at The Lion & The
Rose; Becky Norris at Blackberry Farm;
Carol Hire; Colleen Sikes; Patti and
Gary Wiles at Cumberland Falls Inn;
and Skip Wade and Chris Bryant.

Library of Congress Cataloging-in-Publication Data

Tourtillott, Suzanne J.E.
    Decorating porches and decks : stylish projects for the outdoor room /
Suzanne J.E. Tourtillott.
        p. cm.
    Includes index.
    ISBN 1-57990-207-3
    1. Handicraft.   2. Outdoor furniture.   3. House furnishings.
4. Interior decoration.   5. Porches.   6. Decks (Architecture, Domestic).
7. Outdoor living spaces.   I. Title

    TT157.T63 2001
    747'.8893—dc21   00-063487
                                                              CIP

10 9 8 7 6 5 4 3 2 1

First Edition

Published by Lark Books, a division of
Sterling Publishing Co., Inc.
387 Park Avenue South
New York, N.Y. 10016

© 2001, Lark Books

Distributed in Canada by Sterling Publishing,
c/o Canadian Manda Group, One Atlantic Ave., Suite 105
Toronto, Ontario, Canada M6K 3E7

Distributed in Australia by Capricorn Link (Australia) Pty Ltd.,
P.O. Box 6651, Baulkham Hills, Business Centre NSW 2153, Australia

Distributed in the U.K. by Guild of Master Craftsman Publications Ltd.,
Castle Place 166 High Street, Lewes, East Sussex, England, BN7 1XU.
Tel: (+44) 1273 477374 • Fax: (+44) 1273 478606
Email: pubs@thegmcgroup.com • Web: www.gmcpublications.com

If you have questions or comments about this book, please contact:
Lark Books
50 College Street
Asheville, North Carolina 28801
(828) 253-0467

Manufactured in Hong Kong by Dai Nippon Printing, Ltd.

ISBN 1-57990-207-3

Contents

GRAB YOUR SANDALS AND A COLD DRINK—it's time to head outside. You'll want to be comfortable, so be sure to take a couple of cushions. Better grab a snack and a good book, too. All the comforts of home are just outside your front or back door, in the space between the house and the yard, right there on your porch or deck. This is the place for some serious relaxing, a part of your homestead where no one needs an invitation to sit awhile and just be.

Does your outdoor room beckon to you whenever you have a free moment? Is it an oasis of casual, fresh-air style? Or is it a dusty, under-utilized spot where a broom, a broken lawn chair, and a bag of mulch keep watch over the yard? Do you retreat to the family room, even on the nicest of summer days, because you've never really known how to use your porch or deck to its fullest?

Let us help. We've chosen eight distinctive locations to show you how easy and fun it can be to decorate your own porch or deck with style. The porches reflect a range of architectural styles, from Queen Anne to Bungalow to Rustic, and the decks each reflect a theme that you'll find can work on your deck, too.

The designers and artisans whose work is in this book have contributed their creative best to it, with decorative and functional ideas that will inspire you to see your outdoor room as a whole new part of the house. You'll find most of these ideas will work regardless of your home's particular building style.

We hope to show you not only how to have fun making your porch or deck ready for entertainment and relaxation, but how to transform your outdoor space—whether porch, deck, or tiny stoop—into a place that will delight the senses and lift the spirit. You may find it hard to tear yourself away from your new outdoor retreat.

Introduction

Decorating & Caring
for your porch or deck

IN THIS SECTION, WE'LL LOOK FIRST AT SOME CONSIDERATIONS ABOUT THE maintenance and care of porch and deck floors, before discussing how to best use that outdoor room. Here you'll find tips to help you design an individualized look that suits your needs and shows off your outdoor living space to best advantage. In addition, we've included some practical observations about lighting, fabric, and gardening in pots that will help you create a special outdoor style and mood.

course you'll want to avoid lining everything up along the rails and walls, leaving an uninviting—and unused—bare space in the middle. Make the most of your outdoor living room by carving smaller, more intimate alcoves from the larger space with an imaginative use of furnishings, plants, and decorative pieces.

Before you begin, evaluate the space with an eye for the different kinds of activities that take place there. Why not assign a part of the deck for outdoor cooking and entertaining, while another spot can be a secluded space for reading or relaxing? Outdoor rooms are easily created by physically dividing the space into terraces, using potted trees, large planters, and pots perched on low tables, wide railings, and benches. Remember to try to give every seat a pleasant vista. If you grill, place the stove so that the prevailing winds (usually from the west or south, in summer) send smoke away from seating areas. Don't forget to check out the visual appeal from the inside of the house, too.

The space between the deck's boards is usually small enough to allow you to use outdoor-grade grass mats or sisal rugs, to better define seating areas. These rugs dry quickly and require no maintenance, though you'll need to make sure both sides have a chance to dry after every rain. Remember, too, that large-scale outdoor furnishings feel more appropriate to the surroundings of a deck. If your pieces are on a smaller scale, group them together for greater visual weight. Bring garden-style items, such as metal and weathered wood, outdoors for entertaining or for the weekend—they'll continue to develop a beautiful patina when exposed to sun and wind.

Establishing a Style

Whether you envision your outdoor room as a place to enjoy meals, entertain, or just as a quiet resting spot, what you have first is plenty of potential and opportunity. With a little bit of thoughtful planning, you can tailor the space for any sort of lifestyle or activity, from snoozing to salsa dancing.

GIVE YOUR DECK A FLOORPLAN

If you have a terraced or multilevel deck, you probably already know that you have an entire group of potential outdoor rooms, but more likely you have a large, flat deck surrounded by a waist-high railing that is typical of most modern designs. It can be a daunting decorating challenge (after all, that's a lot of floor space!). Of

PORCH FURNITURE BANNED!

Bessemer City, North Carolina, is thinking about banning the use of indoor furniture on city porches, following the example of nearby towns Wilson and Morganton. One city council member noted a concern that the city maintain a decent image from the moment that visitors enter town. Leave the orange shag rugs indoors, we say.

LIFE ON THE PORCH

There are screened porches, open-air porches, and porches surrounded by glass; whatever your porch, you have an outdoor room just waiting to be transformed into a comfy outdoor getaway and a fine place for plein-air living. Think of the porch as an extension of your living space, snuggled right up to the siding. Of course, we don't mean for you to drag your overstuffed living room furniture out there (see Porch Furniture Banned! at left), but we do hope to bring a fresh garden style right up to the front door. So, gather together some odd lot wood or metal chairs and give them a green-thumb makeover; our Fern & Plaid Garden Chair is on page 63. Unify your unmatched pieces by using a cohesive color scheme.

Because they're protected by a roof, items on the porch don't necessarily have to come indoors when the weather threatens. In fact, a rainy-day lunch on the porch can be just as special as sunning in a lounge chair. Turn your cushions often in high humidity, to discourage mildew. Wicker is not weatherproof, but it is ideal for protected seating areas such as porches. And if you must do paperwork, bring the cell phone, some funky paperweights, and go barefoot. You'll enjoy it more and will probably quit a little bit sooner, while there's still time for some daydreaming.

LIGHTING SETS THE MOOD

Expand the use of your outdoor room by using all sorts of lighting options. The primary light source for evening gatherings may be installed lighting, torchères, or sconces mounted on the house, but don't forget to accent with strings of tiny bulbs; they can be changed or moved in the twinkling of an eye, and make the night feel just a little more special. Once used only at holidays, mini-lights are now considered a year-round standard in outdoor lighting choices. Add bright notes to your outdoor evening festivities by embellishing these twinkly lights, such as we've done with the Moon & Stars String o' Lights on page 94.

Outdoor wiring is great because it lets you drape pretty lights wherever you like, but candles are classic, easy lighting solutions for even the most casual nighttime soirée. Secure a votive with a little melted wax in the bottom of a frosted-glass candleholder; invert it on the deck railing when not in use, to keep rain from collecting in it. Large-scale luminaria, like the Gilded Bugs Luminaria on page 103, can sit on a low bench or light the steps at night. Pillar candles and fresh-cut flowers have a simple beauty that's hard to beat; group them on the dinner table and at seating areas. For evening enjoyment, plant white flowers in pots or in the yard; they have a soft glow you can see on all but the darkest nights.

Fundamental Floor Care

Porches and decks: perfect for long conversations and courtin'—not to mention dining, napping, and twiddling your thumbs. You can get a whole new attitude in the fresh air and sunshine, but before you can really get started with the business of enjoyment, be sure to learn how to prep and maintain that most basic part of your porch or deck: the floor.

WOOD DECK BASICS

With all the hard work that goes into building a deck, you want to be sure the wood is protected so it will meet the test of time. Typically, softer woods are used for decks: cedar, pine, redwood. Pressure-treated woods, which are chemically treated, discolor quickly. Without preventive maintenance, wood will soon look dull and faded, and become home to all sorts of bugs and sludge. A seasonal pressure washing is an indispensable step in preparing a deck for a season of fun and sun. It removes mildew, dirt, and algae, which damage most deck woods.

Use water-repellent preparations, called sealants, and semi-penetrating stains—never latex!—on flat surfaces where water might collect (see Deck Prep Tips, below). Then, once the deck is well sealed, use a long-handled deck brush to promptly remove standing water and fallen leaves.

DECK PREP TIPS

Pressure-treated lumber is chemically treated for outdoor use, but it will still absorb water; adding a water sealer or stain extends the life of the wood.

Before adding a sealer or stain, it is best to remove any mill glaze that may remain on new lumber. To test your wood for the glaze, pour a glass of water onto the deck. After about an hour, if the water soaks into the wood, the glaze has worn off; if the water beads, the glaze remains. A special cleaner is available at most home improvement stores specifically prepared to remove this glaze. Mix the cleaner with water in a 1:4 ratio and work it into the wood, using a stiff brush. Then wash the cleaner away and let the deck dry.

Even if no mill glaze remains on the deck, you should clean the area, in order to kill any existing mold or mildew. Deck washes are sold specifically for this purpose, but a 1:3 water and bleach solution can also be used. As you wash the deck, be sure to scrub the boards well to remove the top layer of wood fibers and give the wood a more even tone.

Next, let the deck dry for a day or two before using the stain or water sealer. Choose a water sealer or stain, depending on the look you desire. Water sealers add a more natural look to your deck. (Remember, pressure-treated lumber often has a greenish tint when it is new, but with weather and time will become lighter.) Stains come in both opaque and semi-transparent varieties. The opaque types of stain are thicker and appear paint-like in texture.

Although pump deck sprayers are available for the application of semi-transparent stains and water sealers, a simple paintbrush or roller more thoroughly covers the wood. Painting the railings with a brush and a roller on the flat areas is generally the most effective method of application. If a second coat of stain is needed, wait for the first to dry before adding it. However, if a second coat of sealer is needed, make sure that the first coat does not dry before applying it. Paint the first coat in one direction, then paint the second coat in the opposite direction.

As a final note, remember to apply the sealer when there is no rain in the forecast for at least 24 hours. After this 24-hour period, your deck should be ready to face any weather.

PORCH BASICS

You'll enjoy a warm welcome at the end of every day—even if your porch is the size of a postage stamp—when the floor has been cleaned and sealed. Concrete porch floors change from drip to zip when they're given the VIP treatment with a soft-toned color stain and sealant—or how about a two-color faux tile look? First, it's important that you correctly prepare the concrete for stain or seal processes. Start by giving the floor a good power wash with a commercial concrete cleaner, using special products for stain removal, if necessary. Pretreat the concrete with acid etching before the application of a sealant, stain, or paint. These come in plenty of beautiful colors that can be mixed to hundreds of tints.

Wooden porch floors offer some great opportunities for creative and colorful treatments. Since they're usually protected from rain and sun, you can paint with abandon. Maybe your porch is ready for some big linoleum checks, or wide, softly colored stripes in subtle shades that complement your exterior paint scheme. Of course, before the painting you should make sure that loose bits of old paint are scraped off first, but this prep work is well worth the effort. Oil-base paints have great wear resistance, and they'll last for years.

Recipe for Neighborhood Fun

Throw a Tom Sawyer party, and ask a couple of neighborhood friends if they're willing to wield some paint-brushes. (Don't forget to return the favor!) Serve Perfect Lemonade and a classic midday Tomato-and-Mayonnaise Sandwich; you'll find the recipes later on in this book.

Fabrics for Outdoors

Whether used for a seat cushion, tablecloth, or canopy, the fabric needs to be tough enough to stand up to the outside elements.

While natural fibers will quickly mildew and fade, synthetic fibers are more long-wearing. The durability of fabric also depends on whether the outdoor area is open or closed. Seat cushions and table runners on a porch will last longer than chair coverings used on a deck.

Luckily, you don't have to compromise your sense of style when shopping for outdoor fabrics. Due to the growing popularity of porch and deck decoration, fabric companies now provide an array of designs and prints for outdoor fabrics; larger fabric shops and outdoor furniture dealers usually carry a wide variety. While no cloth is completely waterproof, outdoor fabrics are water repellent. Solution-dyed acrylic is effective in fending off rain, sun, and mildew. Other acrylics and olefin-and-acrylic blends are also available for outdoor use.

Fabrics made for outdoor use, while quite sturdy, are considerably more expensive than other types of fabric. For a cheaper alternative, vinyl can be treated with spray-on water repellent (available at most sporting goods stores and used for waterproofing camping tents). Look for heavy-duty canvas or oilcloth that sports a modern design. Upholstery fabrics offer another outdoor possibility. Treated with heavier chemical finishing than regular fabrics, they are resistant to dirt, water, fading, and stains.

When mildew growth threatens, brush away loose dirt from the cloth. Using cold or lukewarm water, hose the fabric. Then, with a mixture of water and mild natural soap, wash gently using a soft-bristled brush. After the soap soaks the fabric, rinse and let it air dry. If there are still dirty areas, it is possible to use chlorine bleach and water for spot cleaning, but heavy-duty cleaners should always be used in careful moderation.

With a variety of options for outdoor fabric, you should be able to find something special for your project. Whether making pillows, window shades, or furniture coverings, fabrics brighten up any outdoor living space.

SCREENS & SHADES

If you cozy up to the idea of an outdoor hideaway, you can create a reading or napping nook with screens made of natural materials. Use light and breezy materials that have an open, airy feeling but still impart a sense of calm and seclusion. Bamboo, trellis plantings, and potted trees are perfect natural screens, or you can attach lightweight white cotton or tied bunches of tall grasses to a hinged three-fold open frame.

Freestanding screens are so portable, you can change your arrangements on a whim. If you prefer the convenience of permanently mounted screens instead, bamboo shades are a classic low-key choice, well suited to the style of almost any

home. The Stenciled Bamboo Shade on page 32 changes your plain-Jane shades to eye-catching decorator accents.

HOW TO BE A RELUCTANT GARDENER

Many flowering plants, herbs, and even vegetables can be grown in pots in a sunny spot on the deck. This is especially advantageous if you haven't a lot of ambition or opportunity for traditional gardening pursuits: there's no weeding! Plenty of growing things of all sizes and shapes makes for a lively, inviting space. When the garden extends onto the porch, and your living space expands out into the fresh air, it's like gaining a three-season addition to your home.

Gardens in Pots

Once established, potted plants require little attention. Watering and once-a-month feeding are the two basic needs of container gardens; just use caution: both under- and overwatering are harmful to the plants. It is simple to diagnose an under-watered specimen, because the evidence is immediately apparent when the tips of the plant begin to wilt. Overwatering is more difficult to diagnose, though, because it causes root rot, an invisible but usually fatal condition. When in doubt, water less, rather than more; just don't forget to keep watch for drooping. If you prefer not to fuss with fertilizer solutions, try a slow-release granule feed that only needs application once every six months.

For the truly green thumb–challenged, try a water garden: all you need do is make sure your water plants have the necessary water level (once a week or so). With the addition of a container fountain, you'll enjoy the soothing sounds of a tiny waterfall at your elbow. You can play it safe with hardy succulents, too. They are very forgiving, though with proper feeding, watering, and plenty of sun, some of the most bristly looking cacti will reward you with exotic, long-lasting flowers; some even bloom at night.

Sunny porches and decks are also perfect places to grow small batches of herbs in containers. Terra cotta and concrete planters have a definite advantage over the plastic ones, because they hold the day's heat well. This can be a factor in climates where the day-to-night temperature difference is significant. Warm conditions are essential for growing Mediterranean herbs, such as rosemary, sage, trailing thymes, and oregano; or try an unusual pink, such as dianthus "Sops-in-Wine", and use this perfumed plant to flavor wine and other summer drinks. Even if you don't use a lot of herbs in your cooking, crush a bit of lavender or its cousin, mint, to release its perfume while you curl up with a good book.

Edible flowers are the perfect accompaniment to an outdoor meal, though it is vital that they be grown organically. For this reason, you should never use commercially grown flowers, which are nearly always loaded with toxins. Find spicy nasturtium (*Tropaeolum majus*) or citrusy tuberous begonia (*Begonia x tuberhybrida*) at a well-stocked garden center.

Remember, mildew can easily establish itself around any moist surface, whether paint, wood, or concrete, so keep large pots, flat-bottomed umbrella stands, and boxes off the deck surface; use stand-offs (matching deck pallets), rolling plant stands, or an antique iron grate, so that dampness under them can evaporate.

Green Vistas Wherever You Are

Finally, what about apartment dwellers, with perhaps only a scrap of concrete to call their own? They may dream of wide acres, vast patios, or country porches, but their city stoops—barely big enough to stand on—can nonetheless afford some small pleasure. Invest in a heavy concrete garden planter and stuff it full of your favorite flowers or fragrant herbs. Make a porch angel to hang on the door. Then paint a happy border around the floor's edge, and wait for a butterfly to show up.

Rustic porch

It's easy to see the influence of Cape Cod and French Cottage architectural styles in this shingled two-sided porch, which can generously hold even a large, active family. Simple country pleasures abound here. Meals are taken, stories are told; day turns slowly to deepening blue. The comfort of an old porch will make it hard to leave. When the first cool hint of an early autumn makes you want to stay the day, stretch it out instead. Pile on a sweater and watch the stars appear. Share memories with old friends while the last scents of summer linger on.

Tin-roofed birdfeeder

THE NOSTALGIC LOOK OF AN AUTHENTIC ANTIQUE
TIN ROOF TILE ADDS SOMETHING SPECIAL TO THIS
FEEDER. DECK OWNERS CAN HANG IT FROM A
SHEPHERD'S HOOK THAT CLAMPS ONTO THE DECK RAIL.

DESIGNER:
ROLF HOLMQUIST

INSTRUCTIONS

1 Assemble the roof first; the size of the tin tile will determine the size of the rest of the feeder. Cut a 1-inch-thick (2.5 cm) piece of wood to a size slightly smaller than the size of the tile. For example, if each tile is 12 inches (30 cm) square, cut the wood approximately 8½ inches (21.3 cm) square.

2 Mark and cut the square of wood in step 1 diagonally from one corner to the opposite corner. The two triangular pieces you have will form the roof gables.

3 Cut the cross beam out of ¾ x 1¾-inch (1.9 x 4.4 cm) wood. Again, determine the length by the size of the roof tiles. For example, if the tile is 12 inches (30 cm), subtract approximately 1½ inches (3.8 cm) from each end. The length of the cross beam will then be approximately 9 inches (22.5 cm).

4 Measure and cut the ¾-inch (1.9 cm) exterior plywood to an approximate 14-inch (35 cm) square base for the feeder.

5 Cut four branches to 9-inch (22.5 cm) lengths.

6 Cut four branches to 4-inch (10 cm) lengths. Then, cut each end to roughly a 45-degree angle. These will serve as braces.

7 Cut three branches to 12 inches (30 cm).

8 Place four 9-inch (22.5 cm) posts at the four corners of the 14-inch (36 cm) square plywood. Move them in about ¾ inch (1.9 cm) from the sides, or so that they are spaced to the width of the roof gables. Trace around the circumference of the legs on the plywood, and predrill a hole through the center of each circle.

MATERIALS

2 tin roof tiles of equal size

Wood, about 1 inch (2.5 cm) thick and slightly smaller than one of the tiles

Wood, ¾ x 1¾-inch (1.9 x 4.4 cm) and slightly shorter than one of the tiles

About 12 tree branches, 1 to 2 inches (2.5 to 5.1 cm) in diameter

Exterior plywood, ¾-inch (1.9 cm), 14 inches (35 cm) square

Galvanized screws, ¾-inch (1.9 cm)

Black acrylic paint

Wooden curtain rod finial

2 ornamental pieces of molding to fit in the corners of the roof gables (optional)

Finishing nails

TOOLS

Ruler

Wood saw

Pencil

Drill

Paintbrush

Wood glue

Hammer

To obtain the uniquely rustic appearance of this bird feeder, adapt the measurements given to work with the materials you have.

9 Replace the branches on the plywood. Attach the branches to the base with glue and ¾-inch (1.9 cm) galvanized screws.

10 Set the triangular gable on top of two of the posts. Use a drill and bit to predrill a hole through the gable into each of the posts. Spread a layer of glue on the posts, and use ¾-inch (1.9 cm) galvanized screws to attach the gable to the posts. Attach the gable at the other end in the same way.

11 Glue the braces to the bottom of the gables and the corner posts. Use finishing nails if needed to secure the braces.

12 Position and nail the cross beam at each end of the roof gables.

13 Cut the end of one the 12-inch (30.5 cm) branches at a 45-degree angle. Then cut the branch in half lengthwise. Glue the two halves of the branch to each lower edge of the roof gables.

14 Paint the ceiling tile tins black.

15 Bend one edge of one of the ceiling tiles: use a length of scrap wood to fold over about ½ inch (1.3 cm) of tin. Use a hammer, if necessary, to gently help bend the edge.

16 Predrill and attach the flat tin to the gables with ¾-inch (1.9 cm) galvanized screws. Overlap the bent tin edge over the peak of the gable onto the tin already attached. Predrill, then attach this tin with ¾-inch (1.9 cm) galvanized screws.

17 Paint the curtain rod end and ornaments black.

18 Allow the paint to dry thoroughly. Predrill and screw the curtain rod to the roof.

19 Cut the two remaining 12-inch (31 cm) branches in half. Glue and nail the branches to the plywood base, which will act as a lip to keep the birdseed in the tray.

SCENTED GARDENS

Sweet and mellow, or sharp and exhilarating, how does your scented garden grow? One whiff of a strongly scented plant can become a sweet lifelong memory.

Put these plants in containers around your outdoor space and near windows and entrances so the scents can flow in. Caution: competing scents can weaken the effect!

PLANTS

Banana shrub, black locust, butterfly bush, daphne, eucalyptus, gardenia, lilacs, mint, flowering tobacco, pennyroyal, sweet live, summersweet, true lavender, plumeria

VINES

Carolina jessamine, evergreen and anemone clematis, goldflame honeysuckle, wisteria

Porch angel

WHEREVER THIS RUSTIC
ANGEL HANGS AROUND,
GOOD FORTUNE LINGERS,
TOO. DESIGNER JEAN
TOMASO MOORE USED ODD
SCRAPS OF MATERIALS TO
CREATE THIS DELIGHTFUL
SYMBOL OF WELCOME.

DESIGNER:
JEAN TOMASO MOORE

INSTRUCTIONS

1 Fold the cloth in half. With the scissors, cut the dress shape from the woven material, cutting through both layers at the same time. The dress length from the neck to the base should be approximately 17 inches (42.5 cm), and the width tapers from about 5 inches (12.5 cm) at the neck to 9½ inches (23.8 cm) at the base (see figure 1).

2 Use hot glue to set the stems into place between both layers of fabric, using the shorter flower stems for the arms and the longer stems for the legs.

3 Hot glue the weathered wood piece into place at the tapered end, for the head.

4 Cut two thin strips of fabric, and glue them onto the arm stems to create the sleeves of the dress.

5 To help keep the legs in position and hold the shape of the dress, wrap the 10-inch (25 cm) piece of wire once around each leg.

6 Close up all the openings and seams in the dress with hot glue.

7 Add the feathers onto and around the top of the wooden angel head. Using the twig and the metallic pipe cleaner, form a halo. Glue the halo onto the wooden head, and add any additional embellishment you like.

8 Glue a small flower onto each wrist area, and several leaves for the hands. Glue leaves and small petals onto the bottoms of the legs for the feet.

9 Create the wings by gluing several dried corn husks onto the back shoulder area of the angel.

10 Use the large silk flower to embellish the front of the dress.

11 Screw the small eye hook into the back of the wooden head for a hanging device.

MATERIALS

Approximately ½ yard (45 cm) of recycled woven material (try a vintage tablecloth, lace doily, thrift shop sweater, or any scrap of fabric)

2 silk flower stems stripped of flowers, approximately 20 inches (50 cm) long each

2 silk flower stems stripped of flowers, approximately 11 inches (27.5 cm) long each

Flat piece of weathered wood, approximately 2½ x 5 inches (6.4 x 12.7 cm)

10-inch (25 cm) piece of 18-gauge wire

Feathers

1 twig

1 silver metallic pipe cleaner

2 silk flowers, 1½ inches (3.8 cm) wide each

Assorted silk flower petals and leaves

6 to 8 dried corn husks

1 silk flower, 4 inches (10 cm) wide in a color that complements the dress

½-inch (1.3 cm) eye hook

TOOLS

Scissors

Hot glue gun and glue sticks

Wire cutters

SOLITARY DIVERSIONS

When you have a little time on your hands, solitaire is a great way to pass some idle time. This centuries-old card game was brought to fame through play in the royal courts of 18th-century France. It is known in many countries as "Patience," which is certainly needed if you want to master the game; all you need is a deck of cards and room to lay them out in what's called a tableau. The cards are then sorted into suites according to rules restricting how the cards may be rearranged. Generally, the aim is to segregate the four suites (diamond, clubs, spades, hearts) in descending or ascending sequence, based on the luck of the draw. Play proceeds until the game is won, or until winning is impossible. You may not be alone for long, though; plenty of folks like to do a little backseat card playing.

There are probably more ways to play solitaire than any other game in the world. Find one of the many books on the subject and learn to play a solitaire variation—Klondike, Canfield, accordion, spider, golf, or clock. Solitaire devotees need not be alone; some play double, triple, and quadruple solitaire games, in which two to four players work on their own tableau while using the cards of opponents.

Leather-strapped stool

THIS UNUSUAL RUSTIC STOOL
MAY LOOK LIKE AN EXPENSIVE
GALLERY FIND, BUT YOU CAN
EASILY CRAFT IT YOURSELF IN
JUST ONE AFTERNOON. THE JOY
OF RUSTIC FURNITURE IS THE
FREEDOM TO EXPERIMENT—
WHAT A WONDERFUL WAY TO
SHOWCASE THE NATURAL
BEAUTY OF FOUND WOOD!

DESIGNER:
KEVIN BARNES

MATERIALS

2 wood crosspieces, each 25 inches (64 cm) long and approximately ¾ inch (1.9 cm) in diameter

3 wood legs, each 16 inches (40 cm) long and approximately 1⅛ inches (3 cm) in diameter

4 wood crosspieces, each 19 inches (47.5 cm) long and approximately ¾ inch (1.9 cm) in diameter

1 support with a notched end, 15 inches (37.5 cm) long

Numerous branches for the top, in varied lengths, no wider than ¾ inch (1.9 cm)

Assorted finishing nails, ranging from 1¼ to 2 inches (3.5 to 5 cm) long

Leather strips, for decorative wrapping (optional)

TOOLS

Tape measure

Pruning saw

Hammer

PROJECT TIPS

Brush piles and yard trimmings are good sources for the branches used in this project. City tree services and local power companies may also be able to provide cut branches. The aim is to utilize the resources around you, rather than find exact pieces.

All measurements are for the stool pictured; they should be used as an approximation. When constructing your stool, don't be concerned with minor cracks in the end grain of the wood. Consider such irregularities to be additions to the character of your piece.

The stool is in the shape of a 90-degree triangle, with the 19-inch (47.5 cm) crosspieces serving as the sides, and the 25-inch (64 cm) crosspieces serving as the long side (hypotenuse) of the triangle. The angles do not need to be exact; approximations are fine.

INSTRUCTIONS

1 Collect and select the wood for the various pieces. With the pruning saw, cut the pieces listed and described in the materials list.

2 Construct the frame for the large side: use two of the legs and the two crosspieces 25 inches (64 cm) in length to assemble the hypotenuse side of the stool. Nail the first crosspiece to the legs 1½ inches (3.8 cm) down from the tops of the legs. Nail the second crosspiece approximately 6½ inches (16.5 cm) below the first. When nailing the branches, always select the longest finishing nail possible without the nail coming out the other side of the branch.

3 Turn the hypotenuse panel over. Nail two of the 19-inch (47.5 cm) crosspieces to one side of the hypotenuse panel at an approximate 45-degree angle, in order to form one of the sides of the right angle. You can either achieve this by cutting the branches to fit, or, if they fit naturally, by simply nailing them in place. Keep in mind that the two sides of the right angle must fit together at a 90-degree angle, so cut them to fit if necessary. Use the previously nailed crosspieces on the frame as a nailing guide. Repeat on the other side, and attach the third leg at the intersection of these newly nailed crosspieces.

4 Nail the 15-inch (37.5 cm) support in place. Nail the notched end to the leg on the 90-degree end of the stool, just above the lower crosspieces. Nail the other end to the center of the lower long crosspiece (see figure 1).

5 Nail the smaller stock for the seating in place directly below the top crosspieces. Line them all up parallel to one of the sides of the right angle. To decrease the risk of splitting the wood, leave the pieces oversized when nailing, then trim to size with the saw if necessary (see figure 2).

6 Turn the stool over and repeat the seating procedure, nailing the slightly larger pieces parallel to the other side of the right angle.

7 If desired, wrap the seat with the leather strapping in a manner that is pleasing to you (see figure 3). On the stool pictured, the strapping was wound in and out of the ends of the crosspieces.

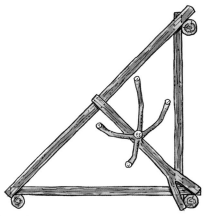

Figure 1

Figure 2

Figure 3

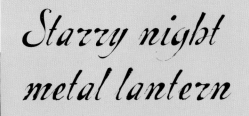

Starry night metal lantern

DESIGNER: **CATHY SMITH**

THIS ELECTRIFIED LANTERN CAN BE CONVERTED BACK TO CANDLEPOWER BY LEAVING OUT THE LAMP KIT. EITHER WAY, DESIGNER KATHY SMITH FOUND AN INGENIOUS WAY TO GET THE LOOK OF 19TH-CENTURY PUNCHED-METAL DESIGN ONTO MATERIALS YOU CAN FIND AT ANY HOME-IMPROVEMENT CENTER.

MATERIALS

Chimney/shanty cap 7 inches (17.5 cm)
    in diameter

7 x 6-inch (17.5 x 15 cm) reducer taper

10 x 12-inch (25 x 30 cm) tie strap
    (thin gauge metal strap, about 1 inch
    [2.5 cm] wide)

Rooftop rain cap, 6 inches
    (15 cm) in diameter

Solvent (acetone or mineral spirits)

Small bolts or machine screws with nuts

Small rubber grommet or washer large
    enough for a lamp cord (optional)

Lamp kit and in-line switch (optional)

Flat glass marbles, ¾ inch
    (1.9 cm) in diameter

Cabinet or drawer pull

60 watt screw-in type fluorescent bulb
    (optional)

TOOLS

Fine-point permanent marker

½-inch-thick (1.3 cm) board, approxi-
    mately 8 inches (20 cm) square

2 C clamps

Masking tape

Small lightweight hammer

Awl

Round log or landscape tie about
    5 x 2 inches (12.5 x 5 cm)

Tin snips

Ruler

Drill with ³⁄₁₆- and ⅜-inch
    (5 and 9 mm) bits

Small screwdriver

Silicone glue

Cutting wheel or hacksaw

Safety glasses

Fine sandpaper for metal

Gloves

Needle-nose pliers

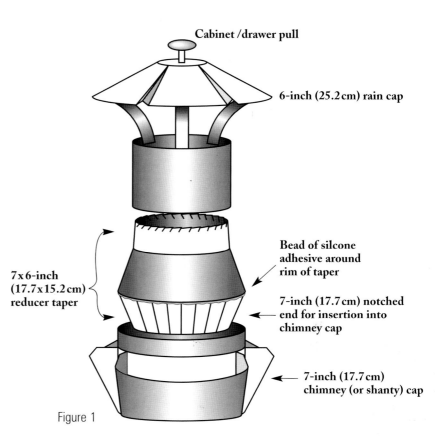

Cabinet /drawer pull

6-inch (25.2 cm) rain cap

Bead of silcone
adhesive around
rim of taper

7 x 6-inch
(17.7 x 15.2 cm)
reducer taper

7-inch (17.7 cm) notched
end for insertion into
chimney cap

7-inch (17.7 cm)
chimney (or shanty) cap

Figure 1

INSTRUCTIONS

Refer to figure 1 for the lantern's
part names.

1 Use the solvent to remove any
labels and glue residue from the
metal materials.

2 Mark your own simple decorative
pattern onto the rain cap with the
marker. Place the board on the corner
of a sturdy surface. Clamp a section of
the cap flat to the board (see figure 2).
Place two or three layers of masking
tape between the metal surface of the
cap and the C clamp, so that the cap
is not scarred by the clamp. With the
awl and hammer, punch the flower
pattern into the metal. Repeat the
process for the remaining sections.

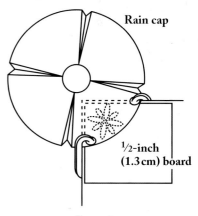

Rain cap

½-inch
(1.3 cm) board

Figure 2

6 Notch the large end of the reducer taper by cutting 1-inch (2.5 cm) strips all the way around it, from top to bottom, so that it fits into the chimney cap. (Otherwise, they are the same size.) Compress these cut strips so the bottom edges slightly overlap and will fit down into the chimney cap.

7 Measure the taper at the widest point and mark the strap. Add 1 inch (2.5 cm) onto each end of the measurement.

8 Cut the tie strap to the proper length. If you do not want the lantern to use electricity, skip the instructions for adding the lamp kit.

3 Screw in the bolts to connect the strap ends to the taper.

4 Drill a hole in the middle section of the taper a little larger than the inner hole of the washer or grommet.

5 Center the washer over the hole inside the cylinder, then use the silicone glue to secure the washer in place (see figure 5).

6 Install the lamp kit according to the instructions on the strap tie. Run the cord through the washer. Install the in-line switch according to the instructions.

3 In order to punch a curved surface, it must rest on a curved surface. Using the round log or landscape tie, slide the metal onto one end (see figure 3). Punch the pattern into the metal with the awl and hammer. Repeat this method for the reducer taper.

4 Using the table, board, and C clamps, punch the patterns into the chimney or shanty cap panels.

5 It may be necessary to trim about ½ inch (1.3 cm) from the small end of the reducer taper, so the leaf pattern will show.

To add the lamp kit

1 Drill a ⅜-inch (9 mm) hole in the center of the strap. It is helpful to drill a ¼-inch (6 mm) starter hole first. Make sure the lamp's threaded end will fit through the hole before continuing.

2 Drill a ³⁄₁₆-inch (5 mm) hole in each end of the strap. Fold the strap ends in 1 inch (2.5 cm) at the proper angle, to fit inside the reducer taper. Mark the end holes, then drill the reducer taper at the marks. See figure 4.

To finish the lantern

1 Run a thick bead of silicone glue around the 7-inch (17.5 cm) rim of the reducer taper. Insert it into the chimney/shanty cap.

2 Weight the top of the assembly until the silicone has cured. Assemble the rest of the lamp. Glue on the flat glass marbles, and allow the glue to cure.

3 Drill a ³⁄₁₆-inch (5 mm) hole in the very top of the rain cap and install the cabinet or drawer pull. If the bolt is too long, use a cutting wheel on the drill to cut the bolt down to ⅜ inch (9 mm).

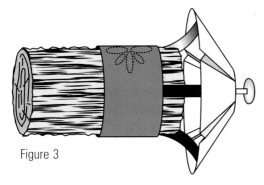

Figure 3

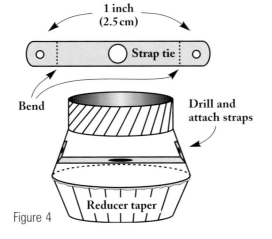

1 inch (2.5 cm)

Strap tie

Bend

Drill and attach straps

Reducer taper

Figure 4

Glue washer to inside surface

Figure 5

STRETCH THE SEASON: HOT SPICED CIDER

Nothing announces fall's arrival like a mug of hot, spiced apple cider. This treat warms you inside and out, and brushes aside excuses for spending less time in your outdoor paradise just because the weather is getting nippy.

SERVES 8

INGREDIENTS

2 quarts (1.9 L) fresh apple cider

¼ cup (25 g) light brown sugar, packed

2 bay leaves

2 cinnamon sticks
    (about 2 inches [5 cm] long)

½ teaspoon whole cloves

½ teaspoon ground cardamom

½ teaspoon grated nutmeg

Zest of 1 orange, peeled in a
    continuous spiral, if possible

INSTRUCTIONS

Combine the ingredients in a large pan. Bring to a boil over high heat, then simmer, uncovered, for 30 minutes. Strain the spices from the mixture and discard. Return the spiced cider to the pan and keep it warm. It is ready to serve. If you prefer, pour 1 ounce (30 mL) of rum brandy or other liquor into each serving mug before filling with the hot cider.

Note: Fresh apple cider is typically not pasteurized. Studies show that most folks cannot taste the difference between pasteurized and unpasteurized cider. But if you like fresh, untreated, preservative-free cider, it can be safely used with minimum preparation. Keep the cider frozen or refrigerated before use. Boil it for at least 30 seconds before use, killing any possible food-borne bacteria.

Bungalow style

Summertime…and the livin' is easy, as the song goes. Porches are natural gathering places for storytelling and comfortable companionship, and this classic bungalow was widely popular with porch-sitters in the late 19th and early 20th centuries. This home's design is based on a French Cottage style that was transplanted to the New World; this particular adaptation features a spacious landing on the outdoor steps. Offer your drop-in guests a tall glass of minty iced tea, and they're sure to linger awhile. If you keep regular porch-sitting hours, you'll soon have plenty of company when neighborhood strollers pass by. What a great place to muse about the weather, or plan your next vacation; but maybe you'll stay home instead…

Stenciled floor border

IF RUGS AREN'T PRACTICAL FOR YOUR PORCH
OR PATIO, PAINT THIS SUBTLE STENCILED
BORDER, DESIGNED BY DERICK TICKLE.

DESIGNER:
DERICK TICKLE

MATERIALS

Clear acetate sheet

White acrylic patio paint

Green acrylic patio paint

Cotton string or chalk line

Exterior clear sealer

TOOLS

Medium-point permanent
marker

Craft knife

Sheet of glass or metal,
for cutting the stencil

Metal ruler

Stencil brush

Palette or plate

Paper towels

Chalk

Low-tack masking tape,
1 inch (2.5 cm) wide

INSTRUCTIONS

1 Thoroughly clean the surface to be stenciled, and let it dry.

2 Measure the floor and sketch a plan using a scale of 1 inch (2.5 cm) to 1 foot (30 cm); a scale plan will help you in laying out the stencil so it fits in the space provided. In order to arrive at a stencil size proportionate for the square corner tile, divide the shortest dimension of the area to be painted by 12 (10 for metric measurements). This figure will be the size of the square.

3 Enlarge the design at a photocopy shop to the size you calculated in step 2 (see figure 1).

4 Trace the design onto the acetate sheet with the marker, leaving at least a 1-inch (2.5 cm) margin at the edges.

5 Using the craft knife, and working over a piece of glass or metal, carefully cut out the tile design. Use the metal ruler for the straight cuts.

6 Repeat the above procedures for the connecting border design, making sure the width of the border design is less than the corner tile. This will add contrast and balance (see photo for guidance).

7 Position the corner tile approximately half the width of the tile from each wall in the corner of the porch.

8 Put some of the white patio paint onto the palette and dab the stencil brush into the paint.

9 Discharge the excess paint from the brush by lightly dabbing it onto a paper towel.

10 Apply a thin coat to designated areas, avoiding too much buildup. Work with a brush that is almost dry. The paint will dry quickly, allowing you to apply the second coat before removing the stencil. If you are using two colors, you may apply the second color now or you may prefer to complete the project with one color first, then come back with the second color later.

11 Carefully remove the stencil and remove any built-up paint from the back.

12 Complete each corner tile the same way.

13 Snap a chalk line from the center of one corner tile to the next and so on until all the tiles are connected with a chalk line which runs parallel to the walls. (Hint: Cotton string makes an ideal chalk line by holding it taut and rubbing it with a piece of colored chalk. You can buy an automatic chalk line from any home-improvement center but it's easy and more fun to make your own.)

14 Mark the center of each chalk line. This will be the starting point for the border design.

15 Position and tape the stencil on the center mark and work away from the center mark toward the corners. This will ensure an even design at each corner. Make sure to keep the center of the stencil directly over the chalk line each time you reposition it.

16 Allow the paint to dry thoroughly, and remove any pencil or chalk lines with a damp sponge.

17 Patio paint is a durable product, but if you want to add further protection apply one or two coats of the exterior clear sealer. Extend the area of the sealer ½ inch (1.3 cm) more than the design.

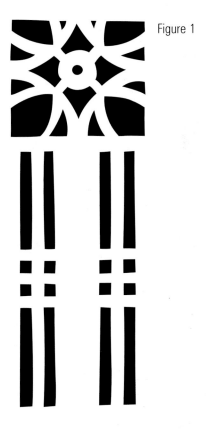

Figure 1

Stenciled bamboo shade

BAMBOO SHADES ARE COOL, CLASSIC, AND SUITED TO ALMOST ANY STYLE OF HOME. THESE GET A FRESH LOOK WITH A BORDER THAT MATCHES THE STENCILING ON THE PORCH FLOOR.

DESIGNER:
DERICK TICKLE

MATERIALS

Bamboo screen

Acrylic patio paint (1 or more colors as desired)

Acrylic exterior clear sealer

TOOLS

Push pins

1-inch (2.5 cm) nails

Tape measure

Long straight piece of 1 x 2-inch (2.5 x 5 cm) wood

Stencils

Palette or plate

Stencil brush

Paper towels

Disposable paintbrush

Water bucket

INSTRUCTIONS

Because the reeds are spaced slightly apart from one another, the intensity of the paint color will be lessened.

1 Before starting the stencil painting, roll out the blind on a large flat surface, making sure the edges are lined up straight. A flat wall large enough to hang it on works even better. The weight of the blind will tend to open out the reeds, and it is in this position that you want to apply the stencil design. If you work on a horizontal surface, use the push pins or 1-inch (2.5 cm) nails between the reeds to keep a slight tension on the blind.

2 Prepare the stencils for the corner tiles and the border design (refer to steps 2 through 6 on page 33 for instructions, using the stencil design pattern from the same page).

3 Decide on how much space to leave between the edge of the blind and the stencil. Leaving a space one-half the width of the stencil usually works well.

4 Use the stencil without using a chalk line. It is better to measure the distance from the edge of the blind as you proceed. Use the long straight piece of wood along the edge of the blind to keep the reeds neatly lined against it.

5 Put some of the white patio paint on the palette, and dab the stencil brush into the paint.

6 Discharge the excess paint from the brush by lightly dabbing it onto a paper towel.

7 Apply thin coats in order to avoid too much buildup, which smears the edges of the design. Instead, work with a brush that is almost dry. The paint will dry quickly, allowing you to apply the second coat before removing the stencil. If you are using two colors, you may apply the second color now; or you may prefer to complete the project with one color first, then come back with the second color later.

8 Carefully remove the stencil and remove any built-up paint from the back.

9 Complete each corner tile the same way.

10 Allow the paint to dry thoroughly.

11 Continue with the border design, repeating it until you reach the corner tiles.

12 Apply one or two coats of the exterior clear sealer, using the disposable paintbrush. Extend the area of the sealer ½ inch (1.3 cm) beyond the stenciled area.

Gardener's porch shelf

THIS PRACTICAL AND PRETTY
UNIT NOT ONLY STORES TWO OF
YOUR FAVORITE GARDEN HAND-
TOOLS, IT HAS SPACE FOR
FLOWER AND HERB POTS, TOO.

DESIGNER:
TERRY TAYLOR

MATERIALS

4 x 4-foot (1.2 x 1.2 m) sheet of
¾-inch (1.9 m) plywood

3 terra-cotta pots, 4 inches (10 cm)
in diameter

7 drywall screws

Latex enamel paint

TOOLS

Pencil

Ruler

Circular saw or jigsaw

Electric drill with ³⁄₁₆- and ½-inch
(5 mm and 1.3 cm) bits

Wood glue

Screwdriver

Router with ¾-inch (1.9 cm)
straight bit (optional)

Sandpaper in medium and
fine grades

Paintbrush

If you have a router, making a ¾-inch (1.9 cm) dado at the bottom of the shelf back will strengthen its construction.

INSTRUCTIONS

1 Measure and mark on the plywood a 6 x 28-inch (15 x 71 cm) rectangle. Cut it out with the circular saw or jigsaw.

2 Measure and mark two slots 1 x 4½ inches (2.5 x 11.3 cm) each; place them 1 inch (2.5 cm) in from each end of the rectangle (use the template in figure 1 on page 38).

3 Use an upturned terra-cotta pot as a template to trace three evenly spaced holes on the shelf.

4 Fit the electric drill with a ½-inch (1.3 cm) bit. Drill a starter hole at the top of each circle and at the top of each slot. Then insert the blade of the jigsaw in the starter hole and cut out the traced circle. Cut out the slots, too, starting from the front of the shelf (the pre-drilled hole will make it easier to turn the corner).

Figure 1

Enlarge 200%

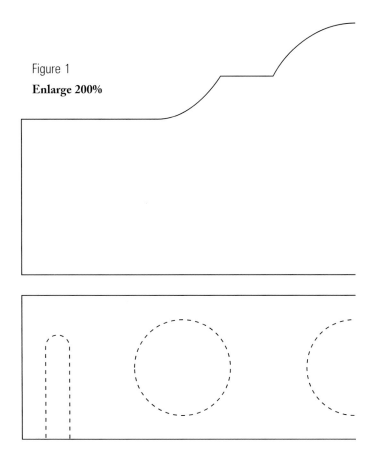

5 Measure and mark a 10½ x 28-inch (27 x 71 cm) rectangle on the plywood.

6 Enlarge and trace the pattern (or simply sketch it) onto the rectangle. Cut the curving edge of the back of the shelf with a jigsaw.

7 Use the electric drill and the smaller drill bit to make five evenly spaced holes in the shelf back, 1¼ inches (3.2 cm) up from the bottom of the shelf back.

8 Spread the wood glue on the back edge of the shelf, then position the shelf on the back. Use the drywall screws to fasten the two pieces together. Wipe the excess glue from the shelf after you tighten the screws, then allow the glue to dry.

9 Sand any rough edges and decorate the shelf as desired. Use a good quality latex enamel paint to cover the shelf. The shelf shown here was further decorated with acrylic paints and rubber stamps.

10 Drill a small hole in each corner of the shelf back. Use the drywall screws to attach the shelf to the wall.

A MATTER OF DEGREES

Porches and decks are favorite locations for enjoying the weather—and for keeping track of it! A properly mounted thermometer offers instant, accurate weather information when and where you need it.

You can go to great expense, purchasing digital instruments that track weather statistics in addition to providing up-to-the-minute readings. Or you can rely on the inexpensive, most commonly used thermometer: the mercury-in-glass type. Invented by Galileo and developed into the modern instrument by Gabriel Fahrenheit in 1714, this thermometer is still effective for backyard use.

THERMOMETER TIPS

Mount your thermometer in a shaded area at least 5 feet (4.5 m) from your home but visible from indoors. Suggested locations: on an interior porch column, under the lip of a deck rail, or on a tree trunk.

Do not mount a thermometer on your home, in direct sunlight, or near water. (All of these can affect temperature readings.)

Regularly clean your thermometer with a damp cloth to remove view-obstructing debris.

Mercury is toxic. If your thermometer breaks, avoid spilling the mercury. Wear disposable gloves to move the unit to a leak-proof container. Dispose of mercury in accordance with local guidelines for hazardous materials.

MATERIALS

8 copper plugs, ¾ inch (2 cm) in diameter

12 copper "T" fittings, ¾ inch (1.9 m) in diameter

Copper pipe, ¾ inch (1.9 cm) wide, cut into 6 lengths of 14 inches (35 cm), for the uprights

Copper pipe, ¾ inch (1.9 cm) wide, cut into 8 lengths of 10 inches (25 cm), for the crosspieces

2 panes double strength glass, 24 x 24 inches (62 cm)

8 pieces of copper sheeting cut in 1½-inch-wide (3.8 x 35 cm) strips that vary in length from 15 to 16 inches (37.5 x 40 cm)

Copper foil tape with adhesive back, ½ inch (1.3 cm) wide

4 acrylic bumpers, ½-inch (1.3 cm) in diameter, available at frame or glass shops

TOOLS

Epoxy suited for bonding copper (available in the plumbing section of hardware stores)

Glass cleaner

Paper towel

Candle

Matches or lighter

Needle-nose pliers

Tin snips

Scissors

Burnishing tool

Copper weave patio table

THIS SPARKLING COPPER TABLE IS AN ELEGANT OUTDOOR ACCESSORY AND REQUIRES NO SOLDERING. DESIGNER TRAVIS WALDREN USED ORDINARY HOME-IMPROVEMENT MATERIALS FOR HER MODERN COMPOSITION.

DESIGNER:
TRAVIS WALDREN

INSTRUCTIONS

Remember to apply epoxy to the ends of each of the pipe pieces before fitting them together.

Making the table

1 Mix a small amount of epoxy according to the manufacturer's instructions. (Continue to remix small amounts as you go.) Place eight of the copper fittings on the ends of eight of the copper plugs. Apply a small amount of epoxy to the open lip of the copper plug and insert it into one side of the copper T. Set it aside to allow bonding.

2 Put the four fittings that have no plugs in them on the ends of two of the 14-inch-long (35 cm) pipes. Set them aside to dry. These are the crosspieces that you will use in step 5. Refer to figure 1 on page 42.

3 Put the fittings on the four remaining 14-inch-long (35 cm) pipes. These are the base and top crosspieces of the table stand.

4 Insert four lengths of 10-inch (25 cm) pipes into the openings of the two base crosspieces that were created in step 3. Repeat this process with the four remaining 10-inch-long (25 cm) pipes for the top crosspieces.

5 Apply epoxy to the other end of the 10-inch-long (25 cm) pipes on the two base pieces. Set these two forms parallel to one another with the plug end down and the epoxied pipe end up. Put the crosspieces (from step 2) in place, perpendicular to these pieces, inserting the epoxied pipe end into the bottom opening of the fittings.

Making the tabletop

1 Clean both sides of the glass pieces with the glass cleaner and paper towel and set them aside in a clean, dry place

2 Light the candle. Holding one of the copper strips in its middle with the pliers, slowly pass the entire length of the strip over the candle flame, making an attractive, lasting color change in the copper. Any soot that forms underneath will be cleaned off later.

3 Heat three more strips using the same technique.

4 Clean any soot off the strips with the glass cleaner and paper towels.

5 You now have four strips of tarnished copper and four strips of plain copper.

6 Now you're ready to weave together the four plain and four tarnished pieces. Place four pieces side by side, alternating the plain and tarnished pieces, and do a simple over-and-under weave with the four remaining pieces, also alternating plain and tarnished.

7 Place one piece of glass on your work surface, holding it by the edges only. Make sure the glass is free of prints and dust. Place a woven piece in the center and "sandwich" it with a second piece of glass.

8 Cut four pieces of copper foil tape, each 4⅛ inches (10.5 cm) long. Peel ¼ inch (6 mm) of the backing away from one strip, exposing the adhesive. Set it aside.

9 Carefully lift one edge of the two glass pieces, maintaining steady pressure to keep the woven copper from shifting. Adhere the exposed adhesive end of the foil tape to the corner, centering it over the edges of the two pieces of glass. Slowly peel away the rest of the tape, adhering it to the entire length of the side of the glass. Trim any excess with the scissors.

10 The tape is wider than the edges of the glass pieces, so fold the extra tape down on both sides of the glass, pressing it firmly, to adhere it to the glass and complete the seal.

11 Apply another piece of the foil tape to the opposite side of the glass in the same manner, then repeat the process on the two remaining sides.

12 Burnish the foil on all four sides and on the edges of the table to ensure a good bond, then clean the outside with glass cleaner.

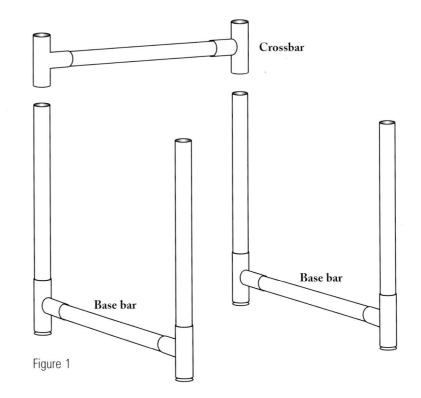

Crossbar

Base bar

Base bar

Figure 1

MINT IN A TEACUP

Mint in a teacup is the quickest way to bring a cascade of green, invigorating fragrance and simple charm to your home. Mint's pleasant aroma, white flowers, and lovely foliage make it a great plant to grow on its own. "True" mints include peppermint and spearmint. Once established, mint is a vigorous grower and will soon have you in the habit of using the leaves in beverages and cool summer salads. Growing mint in a teacup isn't only done for the charm of it: the plant loves to grow and should be con-tained. Mint will quickly spread in open ground. A hardy plant, it is not easily eradi-cated without use of herbicides.

Be creative when selecting your teacup. This is a good time to pull out the chipped china and handmade pieces; old teapots and sauceboats are other excel-lent containers.

Because there is no hole in the cup, the mint will not drain, so avoid over-water-ing. Some mints are climbers that are easily encouraged around the handle.

Queen Anne porch

The strong, repeating pattern of gingerbread ornamentation recalls a Victorian style of architecture known as Queen Anne, or Free Classic. Its gracious porch furnishings speak of a time long past, when lives moved at a slower pace. Welcoming white wicker feels as cool as the sky blue ceiling overhead, and a lazy-turning fan keeps the breeze moving. Every cushioned chair says "stay a spell." Use little distractions to take your mind off the heat: wind chimes and perfect lemonade bring the temperature down to a degree that is downright bearable.

Blue willow mosaic table

THERE'S NO NEED TO DISCARD AN UNUSED
SIDE TABLE AT A YARD SALE. GIVE IT A
BRIGHT, NEW LOOK WITH PAINT AND A
pique assiette ("STOLEN PLATE") MOSAIC TOP
THAT IS PERFECT FOR A COVERED PORCH.

DESIGNER:
TERRY TAYLOR

MATERIALS

Wooden table (preferably one with a raised edge on the top)

Assorted ceramic plates and saucers: 5 blue willow dinner plates for the medallions; 3 or 4 additional white dinner plates are needed for edging and fill-in

1-inch (2.5 cm) square tiles (left over from a remodeling project) can be used as edging

Premixed ceramic tile adhesive

¾ cup (168 g) black sanded grout

1 quart (.95 L) satin enamel paint

TOOLS

Sandpaper

Paper towels or damp cloth

Safety glasses

Tile nippers

2 polystyrene foam trays (such as those used for meat) or similar flat containers

Pencil

Plastic knife or palette knife for spreading adhesive

Plastic container for mixing grout

Disposable latex gloves

Polyethylene foam sheeting (used as packing material)

Sponge or cloth

Masking tape

Small paintbrush

INSTRUCTIONS

Look for inexpensive, chipped blue willow ware at flea markets and yard sales. Vintage patterns in perfect condition can be expensive, but many grocery stores continue to offer this popular pattern, which makes the cost less prohibitive—even if you break them up.

1 Sand all of the table surfaces to remove any pre-existing varnish or finish. Wipe the table down with a paper towel or damp cloth.

2 Use your white plates to practice the following technique before you apply it to your blue willow plates. Wear safety glasses when breaking the plates with the tile nippers. Separate the plates' rims from their bottoms with the tile nippers. Make the initial cut by gripping the plate's edge with the tip of the tile nippers and squeezing the handles together—a large chunk of the rim will break off from the plate. Continue around the plate until the rim is completely removed. On the bottom of most plates is a small foot. Once you have removed the rim, use your nippers to chip away at the foot until it can be removed. If you work carefully, you should be able to trim a nearly perfect circle. Once you feel you have the technique in hand, repeat the process with your blue willow ware. Don't worry if a plate bottom breaks in half; you can still use it.

3 Put the pieces of the plate rims and the plate bottoms in separate containers and set them aside.

4 Place your trimmed plate bottoms on the table's top. Following the photograph, use the plates as visual center points, arranging them as desired. Use a pencil to trace each plate bottom's placement on the tabletop.

5 Use the 1-inch (2.5 cm) tiles for a border. Use a plastic knife or palette knife to "butter" the back of each tile with tile adhesive. Place the tiles around the perimeter of the tabletop; space them to slightly less than ¼ inch (6 mm) apart.

6 Spread tile adhesive on the back of a plate bottom, and position it on the tabletop. Repeat with the additional plates.

7 Use tile nippers to break the white plate bottoms and rims into smaller pieces. Spread tile adhesive on the smaller pieces and use them to fill in the blank spaces between the plate bottoms. Trim small pieces to fit odd-shaped areas, as needed.

8 Allow the tiled area to dry overnight before grouting the tabletop.

9 Mix the grout according to the manufacturer's instructions; it should be about the consistency of mashed potatoes. Wearing latex gloves, use a small piece of polyethylene foam to scoop and spread the grout into the small spaces between

the plate shards and tiles, until the entire surface is well covered. Allow the grout to set for 15 minutes or so, then use additional pieces of foam to wipe the surface clean, removing all excess grout on or between the tiles. Let the grouted mosaic set for 30 minutes, then use a damp cloth or sponge to remove all traces of excess grout and grout haze.

10 When the mosaic has dried thoroughly, mask the edge of the mosaic with masking tape. Apply one or two coats of paint to the table. Allow the paint to dry completely after each coat.

PERFECT LEMONADE

Lemonade. To conjure summer's scent, flavor, and feeling, say no more. And no beverage tops lemonade for simple sophistication. Whether satisfying your thirst on a hot day, or charming your company with its hospitality, lemonade is perfect for all occasions.

Lemonade lovers fall into three categories: tarties, sweeties, and in-betweeners. Any way you like it, the perfect pitcher of lemonade begins with fresh-squeezed fruit. Adjust the following sweet-yet-tart recipe to suit your taste.

SERVES 8

INGREDIENTS

1 cup (.24 L) water

1¹/₂ cups (300 g) sugar

15 to 18 medium lemons, to yield 3 cups (.72 L) of juice

5 cups (1.2 L) cold water

1 lemon, washed and thinly sliced, for garnish

8 small fresh mint sprigs

INSTRUCTIONS

Bring 1 cup (.24 L) of water and sugar to boil in a saucepan, stirring occasionally, until the sugar dissolves. Pour the syrup into a microwavable bowl. Cool. Microwave five or six lemons at a time at a high power setting for 1 to 1¹/₂ minutes (longer for lower settings), until just warm to the touch. Cut the lemons in half and squeeze the juice into a smaller bowl. Discard the seeds and transfer the pulpy juice to a large pitcher. Repeat with the remaining lemons. Stir in the cooled syrup and the rest of the water.

Pour the lemonade into tall glasses over ice cubes. Top each glass with a mint sprig and a slice of lemon. Makes about 2 quarts (1.9 L). Remember to put ice in each glass, rather than in the pitcher, so that the lemonade will be cold and refreshing but not watered down. You can store lemonade syrup in the refrigerator for up to one week.

Wire & bead basket planter

ACHIEVE THE LOOK OF EXPENSIVE CUSTOM PLANTERS BY USING DECORATOR MOSS TO LINE YOUR OWN HANDMADE CREATION.

DESIGNER:
SKIP WADE

MATERIALS

Wire basket, 12 inches (30.5 cm) in diameter

Wire cutters

17-gauge aluminum electric fence wire

34-gauge aluminum wire

3 marbles (cat's-eyes)

Bag of decorator moss

Lightweight potting soil

4 cell packs of assorted colored petunias

INSTRUCTIONS
Preparing the hanging wires

1 Cut the 17-gauge aluminum electric fence wire (this is the heavier of the two wires you're using) into nine strips, each 30 inches (77 cm) long.

2 Hold three of the wire strips together tightly in your hand; wrap a 2-inch (5 cm) strip of the 34-gauge wire six times around the three wire strips, beginning 2 inches (5 cm) in from the end. Tie the ends of the wire together.

3 Working down the wires (away from the newly wrapped end), braid the three wire strips together, creating a 4-inch-long (10 cm) braid.

4 Wrap a 2-inch (5 cm) strip of the 34-gauge wire around the top of the braid six times. Fold open the three wire strips.

5 Place a marble in the folded open wires, then close the wires around it.

6 Wrap a 2-inch (5 cm) strip of the 34-gauge wire six times around the three wires that hold the marble.

7 Wrap a 2-inch (5 cm) strip of the 34-gauge wire around the three wires again, approximately 9 inches (22.5 cm) down from the last wrapping.

8 Repeat steps 1 through 7 with the remaining six 30-inch-long (77 cm) wire strips, creating three wire bands.

9 Hold the three completed wire bands together and wrap them with a 9-inch (22.5 cm) strip of the 34-gauge wire, from the bottom of the wires, completely covering and binding them together. Bend the wires into a hook shape, for hanging.

10 Attach each of the three wire bands by wrapping the unfinished ends (the end opposite the bent hook) to separate sides of the wire basket.

Planting the basket

1 Line the inside of the basket with the sheets of decorator moss, approximately 3 inches (7.5 cm) up the sides.

2 Pour in approximately 3 inches (7.5 cm) of lightweight potting soil.

3 Place petunias around the sides of the basket; plant them so that the flowers are outside the basket, with the root ball on the inside.

4 Line the remainder of the basket with sheets of decorator moss and pour in more potting soil, filling the basket 1 inch (2.5 cm) from the top.

5 Plant the top of the basket with petunias.

Copper oak leaf wind chimes

COPPER AGES BEAUTIFULLY, AND THESE
MELODIOUS WIND CHIMES BECOME
MORE ATTRACTIVE THE LONGER THEY
ARE LEFT EXPOSED TO THE ELEMENTS.

DESIGNER:
TERRY TAYLOR

INSTRUCTIONS

1 Secure the copper pipe in the vise. Using the hacksaw, cut the copper pipe into three lengths of 12 inches (30 cm) and three lengths of 14 inches (35 cm). Set the cut pipe and leftover pipe aside.

2 Secure a length of cut pipe in the vise. Use the hacksaw to cut a 45-degree angle at one end of the tube. Cut the remaining five tubes in the same way.

3 Use the flat or half-round file to smooth the cut edges of the tubes.

4 Secure the cut tube in the vise. Make two parallel holes in each tube by drilling a 1/16-inch (1.5 mm) diameter hole through the tube, 1½ inches (3.8 cm) from the straight edge of the tube. Repeat this step for the remaining five tubes.

5 Using a pencil and compass, draw a circle 5 inches (12.5 cm) in diameter on the ¾ x 6-inch (1.9 x 15 cm) scrap of lumber. Draw a smaller circle, 2½-inches (6.5 cm) in diameter, on the wood.

6 Carefully cut out the circles using a jigsaw. Sand and bevel the edges and sides.

7 Mark the center point and six equidistant marks along the outside circumference of the top face of the larger circle of wood.

8 Drill seven holes 1/16-inch (1.5 mm) in diameter in the 5-inch (12.5 cm) circle: one through the center point and one about ¼ inch (6 mm) in from the edge at each marked point.

MATERIALS

Copper pipe, ½ inch wide (1.3 cm) and 10 feet (3 m) long

Scrap lumber, ¾ x 6 x 12 inches (1.9 x 15 x 30 cm)

Copper sheet (.025 [or thinner] gauge), 12 x 16 inches (30 x 40 cm)

Copper sheet or foil, ½ inch (1.3 cm) wide and 12 inches (30 cm) long

Copper tacks

20-foot (6.1 m) length of monofilament

Metal split ring (used for key rings), ½ inch (1.3 cm) in diameter

2 brass or copper-plated metal beads, ¼ inch (6 mm) in diameter or larger

Note: If you have a sheet metal shop in your town, try asking if you can look through their scrap pile for the copper. Most shops have plenty of scrap they are willing to sell cheaply or even give away for free.

TOOLS

Vise

Hacksaw

Ruler

Flat or half-round metal file

Drill

¹⁄₁₆-inch (1.5 mm) bit

Pencil

Compass

Jigsaw

Scissors

Rubber cement

Tin snips

Awl

Ball peen hammer (optional)

Figure 1
Enlarge 200%

9 Drill a hole in the center of the smaller circle of wood.

10 Photocopy the oak leaf shape. Make four copies, then enlarge the pattern 200 percent and make another copy. Cut out all five patterns.

11 Using the rubber cement, adhere the paper patterns to the copper sheet. Then cut out the leaf shapes with tin snips.

12 File the edges of the leaf shapes smooth with the file. You may wish to texture the surface of the leaves in some manner. In the project illustrated, the designer has hammered the surfaces of the leaves with a ball peen hammer.

13 Drill a hole in the stem of the large leaf.

14 Pierce two holes in the midsection of the small leaf with an awl. Using two copper tacks, attach it to the edge of the large circle. Do not place the tacks at the tip or stem end of the leaf shape, if you want to shape the leaves after assembling the wind chime.

15 Attach all four leaves, overlapping them as desired.

16 Cut a 4-foot (1.2 m) piece of the monofilament, and tie it to the metal split ring. Thread the free end

down through one of the holes on the edge of the 5-inch (12.5 cm) wood disk, back up through an adjacent hole, through the split ring, and back down through the next adjacent hole. Repeat until the monofilament comes up through the last hole; then tie the free end to the split ring. You can level the wind chime easily with this threading pattern.

17 Cut an 18-inch (45 cm) length of monofilament, and thread it through the holes in a tube, then thread one end of the monofilament up through a hole in the 5-inch (12.5 cm) circle and the other end up through an adjacent hole. Tie the two ends of the monofilament with a secure knot.

18 Repeat step 17 for the remaining tubes. After all the tubes are in place, cut off the excess monofilament and slide each knot down in a hole to conceal it.

19 Hang your wind chime on a nail at a comfortable working height to make this step easier to do. Cut a 30-inch (77 cm) length of monofilament. Tie one end to the split ring, thread the monofilament through the center hole, slide a bead and the 2½-inch (6.5 cm) circle onto the monofilament. Slide a second bead below the circle, and make a knot so the bead will hold the small circle roughly in the center of the tubes.

20 Tie the large leaf shape as desired to the end of the monofilament.

TOP TEN VICTORIAN TOYS AND GAMES

10 DOMINOES: *64,000 sets were made in the United States in 1872.*

9 MINIATURE TRAINS: *some even included whistles and gas lamps.*

8 PUZZLES: *in 1850, puzzles with pictures on both sides were patented—leaving puzzle solvers doubly frustrated!*

7 ROLLERSKATES: *with the invention of aluminum in 1870, they soon became a craze.*

6 MAGIC LANTERN SLIDES: *the closest thing to Victorian TV.*

5 ROCKING HORSES: *top-of-the-line models were made with real hide and horse tails.*

4 HOOPS: *even known in ancient Egypt and Greece.*

3 TOY SOLDIERS: *Winston Churchill owned more than 1,500, and always insisted on capturing the French.*

2 CHESS SETS: *some were made to fold over and resemble a closed book. This clever disguise helped clerks and other workers pass the time when the boss wasn't around.*

1 BUILDING BLOCKS: *Princess Victoria herself owned a set.*

PLAYTIME ON THE PORCH

In the days before air conditioning and TV, porches served as a wonderful children's play area. It was in the Victorian era that childhood was first thought of as distinct from adulthood. Along with more playtime, plenty of new toys, such as hoops, were invented for kids. The hoops made especially for younger children had spokes covered in beautiful beads and ringing bells. Others had a musical appliance in the middle that sounded as colorful spokes turned.

Stone & pebble mosaic pot

DESIGNER AMY JOHNSON ADAPTED
TRADITIONAL MOSAIC TECHNIQUES
TO MAKE THIS HANDSOME PEBBLE-
COVERED TERRA-COTTA PLANTER,
USING A DESIGN LOOSELY BASED ON
THE GARDENER'S NEMESIS, THE SNAIL.

DESIGNER:
AMY JOHNSON

MATERIALS

Terra-cotta planter, 12 inches (30 cm) in diameter

Waterproof epoxy

Small white quartz rocks and natural pebbles

Newspaper

TOOLS

Pencil

Rubber gloves

Small paper cups for mixing epoxy

Spatula

INSTRUCTIONS

1 Sketch a spiral motif onto the clay pot with a pencil.

2 Mix small batches of the epoxy and apply it with the small plastic spatula to the design motif you drew on the pot. Make sure to apply the epoxy in a thick enough layer to firmly secure the pebbles. Prop the planter on a base of crumpled newspaper while applying the epoxy, pebbles, and rocks. This will let you work all the way to the base of the planter.

3 Sprinkle the pebbles onto the epoxy and gently press them in, to insure good contact. You may want to do this on a surface covered with old newspaper, so you can collect and reuse any fallen pebbles. Allow the epoxy to fully set.

4 Follow the same procedure to adhere the white quartz rocks to the background. After the epoxy is completely dry, set the planter flat on its bottom and apply the pebbles to the rim.

WHY ARE PORCH CEILINGS BLUE?

Here are some of the more interesting answers:

To keep bad spirits or ghosts away

In the folklore of the South and in tropical climes, ceilings traditionally were painted a special hue called haint blue—a term probably derived from the word haunt.

Because it looks like "sky," wasps and such won't build nests on your porch ceiling.

To keep bugs from your food—they think they are flying into the wild blue yonder.

Green thumb deck

A GARDEN IS A LOVESOME THING.
~T. E. Brown

A green-thumb theme for the deck lets the gardener show off a bit. When the planting is done, it's time to enjoy the fruits of your labors. Nod off in the late afternoon as you congratulate yourself on another successful garden season. Forget the surprise appearance of bugs designed just to munch your roses, and the hours spent spreading mulch. Throw a party, now that your plantings are perfect, and celebrate the growing achievements in your own little Eden. Dazzle your guests with your innovative use of color on the deck as well as off. They'll love you for it.

Tobacco stake potting shelves

RECYCLE AND REUSE HAS NEVER HAD MORE STYLE
THAN IN BILL ALEXANDER'S CLEVER CONSTRUCTION
MADE OF WEATHER-WORN WOODEN STAKES AND
BOARDS. THE MUTED COLOR SCHEME IS RIGHT
FOR ANY PORCH OR DECK DÉCOR.

DESIGNER:
BILL ALEXANDER

MATERIALS

27 used tobacco stakes or other
   wooden stakes, ranging in
   length from 3 to 4 feet
   (1 to 1.3 m)

4 worn picket-fence stakes,
   4 feet (1.3 m) long

3 wood strips, 1 x 1 inch
   (2.5 x 2.5 cm), cut to the
   length of the shelves

4 wood strips, 1 x 1 inch
   (2.5 x 2.5 cm), cut to the
   width of the shelves

3 wooden shelves, sized to
   fit the stakes you use
   (see Instructions note)

65 to 75 wood screws,
   1¼ inches (3.5 cm) long
   (longer screws can be used
   if your materials dictate)

1½ inch (3.8 cm) nails

8 pieces of scrap ¼-inch
   (6 mm) plywood, each
   2 x 3 inches (5 x 7.5 cm)

Wood glue

Small amounts of latex paint
   in various colors

Brad nails

TOOLS

Metal tape measure

Hand saw

Electric drill with small drill
   bit, for starter holes

Screwdriver

Hammer

Paintbrush, 1½ inches
   (3.8 cm) wide

Sandpaper

INSTRUCTIONS

Let the size of the recycled materials you've found help you to determine the final measurements of the shelves and the unit itself. Color the stakes and pickets by painting them with dilute washes of latex paint, sanding them if desired for a weather-worn look.

1 The unit is made from nine stakes on each of the side sections and four pickets evenly spaced among nine stakes for the back section. The pickets begin and end the back section. Lay out the pieces for the back, starting with one picket and three stakes; space them as desired. Measure and cut the two pieces of 1 x 1-inch (2.5 cm) wood strips. Repeat this order until all the pickets are used.

2 Make sure the stake and picket bottoms are even with one another. Lay one of the wood strips across the pickets and stakes, approximately 8 inches (20 cm) from their bottom edges.

3 Use the drill to make starter holes in the wood strip at the position of each of the pickets and stakes. Use the wood screws to attach the wood strip to these pieces, making sure to double check that the screws will not go all the way through the stakes or pickets.

4 Attach the second and third wood strips, approximately 20 and 30 inches (50 and 77 cm), respectively, above the first strip, as you did in step 3.

5 If you have stakes that vary in length, arrange them so the shortest ones are in front and the longest ones are at the back. Measure for the placement of the wood strips on the back section; add 1¼ inches (3.5 cm) to those measurements for the positions of the three side strips. The shelves will rest only on the side strips. Attach the strips to the side sections.

6 Butt the side section to the back section, then join with three evenly spaced wood screws, so the screws pass through the end pickets in the back section, then through the side of the stake. Join the other side section in the same way. For additional support, add wood screws through the pickets on the back into the side wood strips.

7 Set the shelves on top of the wood strips. Tack them into place with hammer and nails.

8 Use the 2 x 3-inch (5 x 7.5 cm) scrap wood to make miniature roof shapes for the pickets. Paint the tops of the pickets with the glue, then nail the scrap wood pieces in the roof shape. Let them dry.

9 Paint the angled wood pieces to match the other wood. Let them dry. Sand with coarse sandpaper so they approximate the weathering on the other wood pieces.

BEE STING RELIEF

Bumblebees are among the least aggressive univited guests you'll meet on the porch or deck. But sooner or later you may find yourself with a throbbing, swelling bee sting.

Unless you're allergic, don't hold any grudges—this mishap is only fatal to the bee, who loses his lower abdomen along with the offending stinger (ouch!). After removing the stinger, wash your wound before trying one of these home remedies for relief of pain and swelling.

TRADITIONAL	FOR THE ADVENTUROUS
Toothpaste	*Ear wax*
Baking soda and water	*Mud*
Meat tenderizer	*Onion slices*
Tobacco (chewed up a little, to make a poultice)	*Vinegar and clay*
	A piece of lean raw meat
Cold compress (a bag of frozen food or ice cubes, or a cloth soaked in cold water)	*Chewed common plantain leaves*

Fern & plaid garden chair

UPDATE METAL LAWN
CHAIRS WITH THIS
STUNNING LEAFY
PLAID DECORATIVE
MOTIF, DESIGNED BY
JEAN TOMASO MOORE.

DESIGNER:
JEAN TOMASO MOORE

MATERIALS

Metal lawn chair

Rust-resistant spray acrylic primer

Acrylic spray paint in light yellow, olive green, and khaki green

Acrylic craft paint to match the spray paint colors

Clear spray acrylic sealer

TOOLS

Wire brush

Sandpaper

Rag

Ruler

Carpenter's square

Pencil

2 rolls painter's tape, 1 and 2 inches (2.5 and 5 cm) wide

Foam brushes

Foam leaf stamps, maple and fern designs (available in most craft stores)

INSTRUCTIONS

1 Prepare the surface of the chair by using the wire brush to remove any rust and loose paint. Sand down the surface to create as smooth a finish as possible. Wipe the debris away with a damp rag.

2 Spray on several coats of the acrylic primer, following the manufacturer's directions.

3 Spray on two coats of the yellow paint as the base color. Allow it to dry overnight.

4 Use the ruler to find the center point on the back of the chair. Using the carpenter's square, draw a vertical pencil line along the center of the entire chair (seat, back, and backside).

5 Attach the painter's tape along the center of the pencil line. Be sure to put the tape along the seat, and the back, and extend it over and down the back side of the chair. Press the tape firmly into place, taking special care to adhere the edges.

6 Measure just over 2 inches (5 cm) on either side of the tape, and once again use the carpenter's square to draw parallel lines on the chair. Tape along the center of these lines.

7 Decide on the spacing of the first set of horizontal lines. The spacing does not have to be uniform, but use the ruler to try to draw the lines as straight and square as possible.

8 Attach the tape to the center of these lines. Press all the tape down firmly, ensuring that the edges are secure.

9 Spray the khaki paint onto the chair. Allow it to dry.

10 Add more tape to the chair, both horizontally and vertically, placing two or three strips in each direction.

11 Spray the olive green paint onto the chair.

12 While the paint is still wet, remove all of the tape, one piece at a time. Allow it to dry.

13 Using a foam brush, apply acrylic craft paints to the foam leaf stamps. Press the stamps firmly against the chair, pulling them away cleanly to prevent smearing.

14 When you are finished stamping, and the paints have dried, seal and protect your chair with several coats of clear protective acrylic spray.

THE NAPPING ESSENTIALS:

Turn off distractions such as the ringers on telephones or pagers. Learn to ignore the doorbell.

Put up any pets that won't be calmly napping with you.

If bugs are a problem, rub on some repellent or light a citronella candle.

Avoid sunburn: get out of the sun, hang a shade or set up an umbrella, or apply sunblock with a high sun protection factor.

For a year-round napping routine, have a blanket handy to ward off chills.

Get comfortable in a hammock, chaise, cot, or chair you can stretch out on. You want to keep your spine aligned and have adequate cushion to avoid putting pressure on joints. Sleep like a pretzel and you could wake up in pain, or find your legs or arms still sleeping from lack of circulation.

Before lying down, make yourself comfortable. Loosen your belt or do whatever's necessary to allow deep breathing during your nap.

OUTDOOR NAP TIPS

Some of us don't need to be convinced of the pleasures and benefits of napping. We define a porch or deck as a private siesta spot. To waste this space would be a pity. (Believers, grab your pillows and blankies and proceed to the fourth paragraph.)

Science tells us a 20- to 30-minute rest during the day offers physical and psychological benefits: increased efficiency and energy, decreased irritation and fatigue. And nappers boast good company. Geniuses like Leonardo da Vinci and Albert Einstein swore by napping for rejuvenation. Even computers are encouraged to doze off when not on task.

In the afterglow of lunch, or perhaps to freshen up for lunch after a morning of reading or weeding, why not settle down for a nap? In Spain, Portugal, and Italy, businesses charge for the use of napping spots. Be grateful you are already at home.

Practice the following tips for securing peace, quiet, and comfort.

Gardener's seed box

THIS STURDY LITTLE SHELF UNIT HOLDS SEED PACKETS, YOUR FAVORITE GARDENING GLOVES, AND SHEARS—WHATEVER YOU WANT HANDY FOR LITTLE EVERY-DAY GARDEN JOBS. THE DISTRESSED SURFACE LETS THE COLORS OF THE OTHER PAINT LAYERS SHOW THROUGH.

DESIGNER:
CHRISTINA BRYAN

INSTRUCTIONS

1 Using a 2-inch (5 cm) brush and paint primer, seal the raw wood; follow the manufacturer's instructions for the primer.

2 Apply a coat of the black paint to the outside surfaces of the wood shelves. There is no need to paint the insides of the shelf areas, because these will be covered with découpage. Let the paint dry thoroughly. Clean the brush for reuse.

3 Apply a coat of one of the two colors you chose; let it dry.

4 Apply a final coat of the second color of paint, and let it dry.

5 Sand the painted areas of the wood so that different colors show through. Use metal tools, such as files, to distress the unit for an antique look. Wipe down the wood with damp paper towels, to remove sanded paint particles.

6 Use scissors to neatly cut out the front panels of the seed packets. If you don't have a lot of seed packets, have color photocopies made of the ones you do have, and use these, too. Plan how the packets will overlap one another by trying out different arrangements before you begin using the découpage medium.

7 Using a fresh brush, apply a thin layer of the découpage medium to an inside area of the shelves that is larger than the size of a seed packet. Lay down the first packet. If you angle some of them so that they extend beyond the edge of the shelf, let them dry before trimming them off with a craft knife.

8 Continue to apply the découpage medium before laying down the seed packets, until you have covered all the interior shelf surfaces. Let them dry.

9 While the découpage medium is drying, keep the brush moist by wrapping the brush in a piece of plastic wrap.

10 The medium dries very quickly; apply multiple layers on the shelf areas to obtain smooth, sealed surfaces. Let each layer dry before applying the next, and clean up any drips with a damp paper towel before they dry.

11 Apply two coats of the découpage medium over the painted wood surfaces to seal and protect them.

12 Add the decorative drawer pull to the front of the drawer.

MATERIALS

Wooden shelves with drawer

Paint primer for wood

1 quart (.95 L) black latex paint

1 quart (.95 L) each of latex paint in two colors of your choice

Paper towels

Assorted seed packets

Découpage medium

Plastic food wrap or sandwich bag

Decorative garden-theme drawer pull

TOOLS

2 foam brushes, 2 inches (5 cm) wide

4 plastic containers to hold small amounts of paint and découpage medium

Medium-grade sandpaper and assorted metal tools, used to distress the painted wood surfaces

Scissors

Craft knife

Carved terra-cotta pot

DESIGNER TERRY TAYLOR ADDED A SUBTLE MOTIF TO THE RIM OF THIS
POT PLANTED WITH NASTURTIUM, BASIL, AND PARSLEY. USE YOUR
IMAGINATION TO ADD YOUR OWN SIMPLE DESIGN ELEMENTS, SUCH AS
THE NAMES OF THE PLANTS, THEIR GARDENER, OR A SIMPLE LEAF PATTERN.

DESIGNER:
TERRY TAYLOR

MATERIALS

Used, broken terra-cotta pot
   (for practice)

New terra-cotta garden pot

TOOLS

Abrasive pad

Letter stencils (bold styles
   work well)

Pencil

Safety glasses

Dust mask

Electric handheld drill

Silicon carbide bits

Disposable paintbrush

INSTRUCTIONS

Carving a design into the rim of a terra-cotta pot is a dusty process. Work on this project outdoors or in a place where the fine orange dust will not cause a problem. It is worth your while to practice using the drill and bit on a broken or used pot. You will learn how much pressure you can comfortably use to carve the letters and designs. Too much pressure makes it difficult to carve and to control the direction of the drill bit. Once you have the feel of the tool, you'll find this is a project that is really quite easy to do.

1 Lightly sand the surface of the pot with the abrasive pad. This helps even out any inconsistencies in the surface color of the pot.

2 Use letter stencils to outline the letters on the garden pot rim.

3 Wearing the dust mask and safety glasses, use the drill and a silicon carbide bit to lightly trace the outline of each letter. Use a light touch to begin carving! Carve several letters lightly before you decide how deeply you want the finished letters to appear. You can always carve away more, but you can't add terra cotta. Don't attempt to make the center portion of each letter as smooth as the pot surface; a roughened texture makes each letter look hand-chiseled. The play of light on the cut surface also makes the letters or design stand out.

4 As you carve each letter, use the paintbrush to sweep away dust from the cut areas.

FLEA MARKET FABRICS

If you're feeling bold, head to the nearest flea market for some funky fabric finds. Because everything is sold at bargain prices, this is a great time to take some decorating risks. That old green and orange chenille bedspread might make the perfect porch pillow. Perhaps those bright yellow curtains can become a cheerful picnic cloth. Let your creative spirit loose as you search for the next treasure.

Dedicated flea market shoppers are up at the crack of dawn, so arrive early for the best finds. Bring a set of room photos or fabric swatches if you're matching other colors; the hunches that don't work can be sold at your next garage sale.

Remember, negotiating the price is usually acceptable, so here's a chance to sharpen your bargaining skills. Take cash in small bills, too. You don't want to find a beautiful embroidered tablecloth and be stuck without change!

Some of the fabrics might not be in top condition, but you can easily spruce them up. Try testing a commercial stain remover on a less obvious part of the fabric first, when removing stains. For spots of gum or sticky substances, freeze the fabric and then gently scrape them off. With yellowed or heavily soiled fabrics, presoak for no more than half an hour in bleach or detergent, then rinse before laundering. After washing in cool water, the fabric is ready for use.

Flea market shopping is an escapade in itself, and you can take advantage of funky flea market bargains to step out and try new things with them.

Victorian lover's porch

The perfect stillness of a glassed-in porch, when the room holds sunshine for a magical hour or two, is caught in this light-filled turn-of-the century Victorian retreat. Make it as private or public as you like; throw the doors wide, or hang gauzy half-curtains to diffuse the landscape. Breakfast becomes a special event when you're surrounded by sparkling panes of glass and the dawning colors of the day, and on moonlit nights you can trip the light fantastic as the two of you do a moonlit tango, accompanied by the recording of a scratchy orchestration from a bygone era.

Tea-dyed leafy curtains

GAUZE CURTAINS ARE PERFECT SUMMERTIME
ACCESSORIES, INDOORS OR OUT. DESIGNER TRAVIS
WALDREN SCATTERED DELICATE DETAILS FROM
FRESH LEAVES OVER THESE SHEERS.

DESIGNER:
TRAVIS WALDREN

INSTRUCTIONS

1 Collect fresh, green leaves from nature, or use patterns traced from pattern books. Use the permanent ink pens to trace the leaf designs on the face of the curtains. Include any veins for a detailed, realistic look.

2 Fill in the leaves using the colored fabric pens or diluted fabric paint. Let the curtains air dry.

3 Use the fine black pen to redraw the details and the edges of the leaves.

4 Iron the curtain with a moderately hot iron.

5 Put the tea bags in the washing machine and fill the machine with hot water.

6 Allow the tea bags to steep, then add the curtains for five to ten minutes, depending on the intensity of color you want. Remove the tea bags, then rinse the curtains in cold water and hang them to dry.

MATERIALS

Leaf designs (real leaves or designs from pattern books)

Two gauze curtains, approximately 36 x 64 inches (1 x 1.6 m)

Waterproof and fade-proof permanent ink pens, in an assortment of browns and greens

Colored fabric pens or fabric paint

Black fine-tip permanent ink pen

12 black tea bags

TOOLS

Iron

Washing machine

LIFE'S LITTLE PLEASURES

It's the simple things in life that are worth treasuring, and who doesn't love tomato-and-mayonnaise sandwiches? They're quick and satisfying—summer between two pieces of bread!

Tomato-and-Mayonnaise Sandwiches

INGREDIENTS

Vine-grown tomatoes,
*   1 per person*

Boston bibb lettuce

Mayonnaise

Fresh and fluffy white bread

INSTRUCTIONS

Tear whole lettuce leaves from the core and rinse them in a colander. Put all the leaves in a large kitchen towel and shake repeatedly to remove most of the moisture. Slice the tomatoes with a long, serrated knife. Spread plenty of mayo on the bread, and enjoy.

If you're really adventurous, try one of these oddball sandwich combos.

I like peanut butter and bananas and potato chips, is that strange? The chips give it a nice crunch. ~Kathy

Peanut butter, jelly, and potato chips on wheat. Okay, so it's not so strange. So, shoot me. ~Joe

Ever since he was a kid, one of my brother's favorite sandwiches has been sausage and grape jelly on toasted bread. ~Tom

How about potato salad, dill pickle and chopped egg on rye? Yum. ~Dana

Pressed autumn leaves & grasses

THE BEAUTY OF YOUR GARDEN FAVORITES
SHINES THROUGH IN THESE UNIQUE PIECES.
DESIGNER LOVEETA BAKER LETS THE SUN
ADD ITS OWN DECORATIVE TOUCH.

DESIGNER:
LOVEETA BAKER

MATERIALS
to make 1 frame

2 panes of glass, same size
   as the frame's inner
   measurementss

Leaves, grasses, feathers, or
   pressed flowers (preserve
   the leaves by spraying with
   several light coats of clear
   acrylic spray)

Picture frame

Fabric and/or paper scraps

Paint or stain for frames

Turn buttons (these plastic
   pieces screw into wood
   frames; find them at
   hardware stores)

Screw eye or nails

Monofilament line

TOOLS

Heavy book

Paintbrush

INSTRUCTIONS

1 With the empty frame laying on a
flat work surface, experiment with
laying out various arrangements of
the collage materials (leaves, grass,
paper, fabric, etc.).

2 Once you have a composition that
you like, clean the glass and lay the
first pane down on the work surface.
It may help to put a sheet of white
paper under the glass, to add some
contrast to the materials. Position the
composition on the glass, then place
the second sheet of glass over the top.

3 Put a heavy book or two on top of
your work for approximately one
hour, to press the objects flat.

4 While waiting, paint or embellish
the frame if you like.

5 Attach the turn buttons to the
frame. Make certain they won't
show through to the front by placing
them close to the outside edge of the
frames. If you are using a narrow
frame, you may need to use thumbtacks instead.

6 Drive in the screw eyes and attach
the hanging wire or monofilament. Do not drill or hammer on the
frame after the glass is installed!

7 Now that the composition is
pressed and the frame is ready,
carefully place the glass into the
frame, and secure it with the turn
buttons (or position the thumbtacks
at the inside edge of the frame to
hold the glass in place).

Fresh-cut flowers brighten spaces and lighten spirits. We snip them and set them in vases to savor their beauty and fragrance. Then the sweet peas start slumping. Lilies look limp. Yes, at some point daisies do droop, but you can help your fresh-cut flowers resist the inevitable with a little effort. Fresh-cut flowers on the porch, deck, or indoors need water, shade, and nourishment if you expect them to last more than a couple of days.

USE THE FOLLOWING TIPS:

Pick the freshest flowers—tight buds with healthy leaves.

Recut stems on a slant under lukewarm water.

Remove bruised leaves and foliage that fall below the waterline in your vase.

Float stems in warm water in a dark, cool place for several hours before arranging.

Would you drink from a dirty glass? Don't expect your flowers to! Bacteria spells early death for fresh-cut flowers. Wash your vase before each use.

Place your arrangement in a cool spot out of the sun. Change the water every other day.

When blooms wilt, recut their stems under water.

Flowers can also be kept in a cool room or refrigerator when they're not on display, away from uncovered fruit and vegetables that spread decomposing bacteria.

Flower food containing sugar, an anti-bacterial agent, and an acidifier (to prevent the stem end from closing and cutting off the water supply) will lengthen a life span. Use this simple recipe:

    1 cup (200 g) citrus soda
    1 cup (.24 L) water
  1/2 teaspoon (2.5 mL) household bleach
       (Increase proportionally to fill the vase.)

KEEP FRESH-CUT FLOWERS FRESH

Using these tips, try your hand at extending the vase life of these popular, hearty varieties of fresh-cut flowers:

ASTERS, *sometimes called a "bouquet of one," flower in all colors but orange. Vase life: 1 to 2 weeks*

COSMOS *resemble lace and are adored by butterflies. Vase life: 5 to 6 days*

GYPSOPHILA, *a.k.a. baby's breath, feature starry blossoms on delicate stems. Vase life: 5 to 8 days*

RUDBECKIA *often grow wild and are called coneflowers and black-eyed Susans. Vase life: 7 to 14 days*

SCABIOSA *are densely petaled mounds of blossoms called starflowers, and are favored by butterflies. Vase life: 5 to 7 days*

SNAPDRAGONS *offer spires of blossoms that come in every shade but blue. Vase life: 7 to 14 days*

STATICE *feature rainbow colors. Vase life: up to 2 weeks*

SUNFLOWERS *guarantee sunshine. Vase life: up to 1 week.*

ZINNIAS *are easy to find and come in a variety of shapes, sizes, and colors. Vase life: 5 to 10 days*

Tea towel pillows

SIMPLE PILLOWS, IN TERRY
CLOTH AND OTHER STURDY
FABRICS, HAVE A PRACTICAL
STYLE WELL-SUITED FOR
OUTDOORS. SUSAN KINNEY
USED A COLOR SCHEME
REMINISCENT OF A LATE-
SUMMER VINEYARD FOR
HER THREE DESIGNS.

DESIGNER:
SUSAN KINNEY

Five-button woven cloth envelope pillow

INSTRUCTIONS

You may want to make nonstandard-size pillows, which require that you use stuffing instead of pillow forms. See How to Make a Muslin Case, page 80.

1 Fold over the woven tea towel so the seams are together and a flap is formed. Stitch the two sides together. Turn the pillow right side out.

2 Turn in the sides of the flap, and hem them by hand with a needle and thread.

3 Stitch the piping to the open flap.

4 Attach the one large and four small buttons to the flap in a row parallel to the flap's edge.

5 Stuff with the pillow form or the muslin cased stuffing (see How to Make a Muslin Case, page 80).

6 Attach the hook-and-eye strip to the inside of the flap's edge, and also to the corresponding area on the pillow's front.

Three-button woven cloth pillow

INSTRUCTIONS

1 Cut out the back and front pieces from a woven tea towel, adding ½ inch (1.3 cm) for seams. Reserve the leftover pieces for the terry cloth tea towel pillow.

2 Cut a length of piping equal to the length of the four sides of the material you cut in step 1.

3 Sew together three sides of the woven material with the piping (facing to the inside) between them, leaving a short side open. Turn the pillow right side out.

4 Attach the contrasting solid color buttons to the center of the pillow.

5 Stuff with the pillow form or the cased stuffing.

MATERIALS
To make two woven cloth pillows

2 woven tea towels

2 feet (62 cm) of adhesive-backed hook-and-loop tape, ½ inch (1.3 cm) wide

Cotton/poly thread, in a color that complements the towels

Piping to match the buttons—the length needed is determined by the pillow size

3 solid-color buttons that complement the towels

1 larger and 4 smaller buttons in a color that complements the towels

Pillow form

TOOLS

Sewing needle

Scissors

Tape measure

Sewing machine

Terry cloth pillow

ADDITIONAL MATERIALS

2 contrasting terry cloth tea towels, in colors similar to the woven tea towels

1 woven tea towel, to match the towels used for the other pillows

INSTRUCTIONS

1 Determine the pillow size based on the size or pattern of the towel, or the shape of your pillow form.

2 Cut out back and front shapes for the pillow, adding ½ inch (1.3 cm) for the seams. Cut a small center square, one-half the size of the pillow, in a coordinating color of terry cloth.

3 Cut four pieces from the finished edges of a woven tea towel for the flanges, adding ½ inch (1.3 cm) for seams. A flange is a decorative piece of flat material used the same way as piping. Refer to the photo, noting that these flanges are short, stopping at the corners of the pillow rather than turning them.

4 Sew three of the pillow's sides together, with the finished edges of the flanges facing in. Turn the pillowcase right side out. Insert the pillow form or stuffed muslin case.

5 Finish the last side by hand, hemming it in with the last flange.

6 Hand stitch the coordinating terry cloth pattern square into the center of pillow.

How to make a muslin case

MATERIALS

Muslin for case

Polyester pillow stuffing

Thread

TOOLS

Sewing machine (optional)

Needle

INSTRUCTIONS

1 If you're using polyester stuffing instead of a pillow form, make a quick muslin case for it. Cut a piece of muslin the same width but double the length of the finished pillow, adding a ½ inch (1.3 cm) for a seam allowance.

2 Fold the long side in half, then sew two of the three open sides closed. Turn it inside out, then stuff with the polyester stuffing.

3 Hand stitch the third side closed.

A LITTLE PORCH MUSIC, PLEASE

It may look good and feel good, and what you serve there may smell and taste good, but your porch is not complete without melodious sound. Your porch or deck can be a place to make and share music, whether as a solitary pursuit or when you're socializing.

Time spent alone is an opportunity to practice and test musical skills you might not have the guts to share with company. And that's just fine.

Most instruments lend themselves to solo porch music, including your voice, acoustic guitar, ukulele, dulcimer, cello, fiddle, harmonica, harp, banjo, clarinet, mandolin, spoons, trumpet, tambourine, and saw blade. Amplified instruments, such as electric guitars or basses, and drum kits, are best reserved for folks without neighbors.

If entertaining is on your mind and you simply cannot play any of the above, give thought to where your "packaged" music comes from. A portable radio plugged into an exterior outlet, or fed current with an extension cord, brings music outdoors, but it doesn't provide much freedom of choice, high-quality sound, or atmosphere. A full stereo

system that plays cassettes, compact discs, vinyl albums—even eight-tracks or reel-to-reel—lets you reminisce and move around the history of recorded music.

Though multi-disc players provide a steady stream of beats for hours on end, this can downgrade the music to mere backdrop. That won't be the case if you pull out your old LPs, 78s,

and 45s. These recordings require attention—someone to lay or lift the needle and pick the next song.

Humidity and sunshine will damage all your music sources—recordings, equipment, and instruments alike—so bring all your music-making stuff indoors when it's not in use. When using electronics, keep cords and antenna safely out of the way.

Coppery lichen wreath

DESIGNER JEAN TOMASO MOORE CONTRASTED THE ROUGH TEXTURE OF LICHEN-COVERED TREE BARK WITH THE CONTEMPORARY ELEGANCE OF METALLIC RIBBON AND WIRE, MAKING THIS SIMPLE WREATH AN ATTRACTIVE ACCENT FOR THE HOME.

DESIGNER:
JEAN TOMASO MOORE

MATERIALS

Lichen-covered bark

19-inch (47.5 cm) straw wreath form

Dried green moss

1 spool of 18-gauge copper wire

2 lichen-covered branches

Several 1-inch (2.5 cm) copper-plated nails

2 yards (1.8 m) copper-colored French wire ribbon, 2 inches (5 cm) wide

1 yard (.9 m) copper-colored French wire ribbon, 1 inch (2.5 cm) wide

TOOLS

Hot glue gun and glue sticks

Chopstick or other pointed tool

Wire cutter

Hammer

INSTRUCTIONS

1 Gather lichen-covered bark from a fallen tree.

2 Cover the wreath with bark, using hot glue to adhere it. Choose pieces that conform to the curves as much as possible, breaking the bark into smaller pieces if necessary.

3 When the entire front and side surfaces are covered, check for any gaps or exposed areas where the original wreath form is still visible. Insert moss into any open crevices. Dab in a little glue and poke moss into the opening, using the chopstick to push it into tight spaces.

4 Wrap the ends of the branches in copper wire to add a modern design element to the rustic quality of the wreath.

5 Experiment with the branch placement to find an aesthetically pleasing position. Using the hot glue gun, attach it to the wreath at the points where the branch and bark will touch. Hammer one or two copper nails through each end of the branch into the bark.

6 Create a bow with the 2-inch (5 cm) ribbon. Fold the 1-inch (2.5 cm) ribbon in half to create a streamer. Dab hot glue at the fold and tack it onto the underside of the bow.

7 Attach the bow to the wreath with hot glue, draping it behind the branches.

Dining al fresco

Even a modestly sized modern deck can be transformed from everyday utility to a cozy dining
alcove. Keep a brightly painted wood table outdoors for impromptu dinner parties. There's something about dining outdoors that makes food taste
better and makes the meal more festive. The term
al fresco comes from the Italian, meaning "in the
fresh air." When the mere thought of eating hot
food raises your heat index, dream up a refreshing
cold dinner instead. Pack the necessities and
accessories that you'll need into oversize baskets
for fewer trips back to the house. Take plenty of
candles, nice stemware wrapped in cloth napkins,
and tiny bottles of chilled sparkling water in striking
shapes and colors (pop a few fresh flowers in one
of them). Play it loose; the idea is to enjoy yourself
because you're out of the kitchen.

Leafy green napkins

THE NATURAL BEAUTY OF FRESH GREEN
LEAVES ADORNS THESE DINNER NAPKINS.

DESIGNER:
KATHY COOPER

MATERIALS

Green leaves of any type

Heat-set photo transfer sheets

Cream-colored napkins

Gold acrylic paint

TOOLS

Scissors

Clean cotton cloth

Iron

Disposable plate

Sponge stamps in square and
dot shapes

INSTRUCTIONS

1 Lay the leaves directly on the copy glass of a color laser copier, arranging them in the most efficient way possible so you don't waste any of the transfer paper. Over this, lay a sheet of paper as close to the color of the napkins as possible; do this so the small border you'll be cutting around each leaf blends in with the color of the napkin. After proofing the design as a color photocopy, have the copier technician load the copier with heat-set photo transfer sheets and make the copies.

2 Back home, cut out each of the leaves from the photo transfer paper, following the shape closely and leaving a small, even border around each one.

3 Randomly place the leaf cutouts, facedown, on each of the napkins. Cover the napkin with a clean cotton cloth.

4 On a hard surface, such as a countertop, use a hot, dry iron to transfer the cutouts. Use firm pressure as you iron. Peel off the backing material while it's still warm, and let the transfers cool a moment.

5 Pour the gold paint into the disposable plate. Dip the stamp into the paint and print a pattern of squares around the perimeter of the napkins.

6 Stamp dots randomly onto the napkins.

CATCHING FIREFLIES:
THE WHERE, WHEN & HOW

Fireflies light up the night with their bright, blinking lights before disappearing into the black, and here's the where, when, and how of catching these fascinating beetles. The common names of firefly or lightning bug describe various winged nocturnal beetles that emit intermittent lights ranging from yellow to red-orange. Their lights are signals between males and females hoping to reproduce.

With more than 1,000 species worldwide, fireflies are most commonly seen during late spring and summer nights. They are attracted to low, overhanging trees and tall grasses, which give them a place to rest out of the sun in daylight. Look for fireflies on the edges of woods, in fields, and in lush gardens. They prefer to save their blinking for the darkest nights, when their light will be the most obvious to a possible mate. Full-moon nights are generally not good for firefly catching, although desperate fireflies will be seen.

The flashes—from males about every five seconds—originate from the beetle's abdomen, where oxygen reacts with chemicals to produce light. Females, which stay on the ground, flash only in response to males, generally two seconds after. This come-hither is crucial to both male and female fireflies, who generally live only a few weeks.

Fireflies may be gently caught by hand and stored in a see-through container with a lid punctured to allow airflow. Don't keep them for long, because captured fireflies generally decrease their blinking while plotting their escape and when potential mates are out of sight.

Icy wine bucket

THE WINE STAYS CHILLED ON THOSE
HOT SUMMER NIGHTS IN THIS BUCKET
MADE OF ICE AND GRAPEVINES.

DESIGNER:
SKIP WADE

INSTRUCTIONS

1 Fill the 3-liter soft drink bottle with approximately 1 inch (2.5 cm) of water, and put it in the freezer until solidly frozen.

2 Fill the 1-liter soft drink bottle with sand, and set it inside the 3-liter bottle, centered on top of the frozen layer.

3 Add about a ½ inch (1.3 cm) of cold water in the space between the two bottles, and freeze again. This joins the bottles.

4 Arrange grapevines between the two bottles from bottom to top (let some vine ends stick out at the top).

5 Fill the space with cold water, about ½-inch (1.3 cm) from the top, and freeze until solid. Empty the sand from the 1-liter bottle.

6 To remove the inside bottle, fill the smaller bottle with warm water and quickly pull it from the ice mold.

7 Use the sharp knife to cut down the sides of the 3-liter bottle, to aid the removal of the ice mold. Return the ice bucket to the freezer until you're ready to use it.

8 To use, set the ice bucket in a shallow dish or bowl to catch water as the bucket melts. Decorate the base with left-over vines or flowers, then place the wine bottle in the bucket.

MATERIALS

3-liter plastic soft drink bottle, with the rounded top section and mouth cut off

1-liter plastic soft drink bottle, with the rounded top section and mouth cut off

Play sand, enough to fill the 1-liter soft drink bottle

Grapevines—or any vine, leaf, or flower

TOOLS

Sharp knife

MATERIALS

20-gauge copper sheet stock

4-inch (10 cm) length of 1½-inch (3.8 cm) diameter brass or copper pipe

Liquid flux

Spool of soft solder

¼ x ⅛ inch (6 x 3 mm) copper or bronze nail

Denatured alcohol

TOOLS

Metal scriber or fine-tipped permanent marker

Metal shears

Medium grade metal file

Synthetic abrasive potscrubber pad or medium-grade steel wool

Hardwood salad bowl, at least 6 inches (15 cm) in diameter, or dapping block

Shallow wooden box filled with sand

Ball peen hammer

Hacksaw with fine-toothed blade

Plastic-bristle paintbrush, cut to ¼ inch (1 cm) in length, to apply the flux

Asbestos pad or other heatproof surface, such as brick or concrete

Safety glasses

Electric soldering iron

2 short pieces of scrap lumber

Vise

Flat-nosed pliers

Rubber mallet

Masking tape

Clean rag

Fine steel wool

Brass & hammered copper candleholder

LIGHT UP A ROMANTIC AL FRESCO DINNER
WITH THE GLEAM OF CANDLES, USING
DESIGNER MICHAEL SAARI'S SUBTLE HAMMERED-
METAL TECHNIQUE TO ADD TEXTURE TO THIS
OUTSTANDING CANDLEHOLDER.

DESIGNER:
MICHAEL J. SAARI

INSTRUCTIONS

Copper is a very soft metal, and is easily bent to any shape. Use an electric soldering iron, and be sure to follow the manufacturer's instructions for it—including their recommendation for the type of solder to use.

1 Use the scriber to trace two 6-inch (15 cm) circles onto the copper sheet.

2 Using the metal shears, cut the two disks from the copper sheet. Use the file, then follow with the potscrubber pad or steel wool to smooth the sharp edges of the disks.

3 Set the salad bowl into the box of sand. You will make the dish-shaped top and bottom pieces by sinking (hammering) the copper disks into the shape of the bottom of the bowl. It is easier to start hammering the disk on the inner side of the bowl, moving it down into the bottom as it begins to follow the bowl's shape. Use a soft, regular tapping motion of the ball peen hammer, working outward from the center.

4 Using the hacksaw, cut a 4-inch (10 cm) length of pipe. This piece will connect the two hammered disks.

5 Set one of the curved copper disks facedown on a flat surface. Use the scriber to trace around the pipe's opening onto the back side of the curved disk. Repeat for the other disk.

6 On one of the disks, paint a line of flux just inside the line you scribed.

7 Place the disk onto the asbestos pad and put on the safety glasses. Extend a short length (approximately 4 inches [10 cm]) of solder out from the spool of solder. Working on the asbestos pad, spot solder one of the disks to the piece of pipe to secure their positions. Remember that solder will not fill gaps, so the two pieces must touch at all points. The solder becomes a decorative element; it will not match either the brass or the copper.

8 Now solder the two pieces completely where they meet. Repeat step 7 to attach the second disk to the other end of the copper pipe. Finish joining the second disk as you did the first one.

9 For the handle, cut a tapered piece of copper sheet that is 12 inches (30 cm) long, 1½ inches (3.8 cm) wide at one end, and 1⅛ inches (3.2 cm) at the other.

10 The long sides of this tapered piece will be folded in toward the center. Sandwich the tapered piece between two short pieces of lumber, so that a 3/16-inch (5 mm) piece of the long side extends out from their edges. Put these pieces lengthwise in a vise.

11 Using the flat-nosed pliers or a rubber mallet, bend the exposed strip of metal down to the wood, so it forms a 90-degree angle. On a flat surface, use the rubber mallet to bend this angle down, so it is folded flat to the metal. This eliminates the sharp edges and makes the handle stronger and more rigid.

12 Repeat step 11 for the other long side of the handle piece.

13 At the wider end of the handle piece, use the flat-nosed pliers to bend a 2-inch (5 cm) loop onto itself, to make the handle. At the other end, bend a curve to fit the bottom of the candle stand (see photo on page 90).

14 Use masking tape to hold the handle in position on the center piece; keep the tape away from where the loops touch the center piece. Spot solder these loops onto the center piece.

15 Spot solder the copper or bronze nail to the center of the inside of the top disk; this prevents the candle from slipping.

16 Use denatured alcohol and the potscrubber pad to clean the soldering flux residue. Wipe the piece clean with a cloth rag.

17 Use the steel wool to shine the piece.

MIDNIGHT GARDEN DELIGHTS

No, nightbloomers are not what you wear to bed, they're moonflowers and moonvines, a rare variety of flowering plants with a loyal following. Connoisseurs stay up late (or rise early) to watch moonflowers' white blooms open during late evening hours, then close before dawn breaks.

Part of the morning glory family, moonflowers (*genus calonyction*) are tropical American plants, often heavily fragrant. Their flowers are much larger than those of morning glories. It is theorized that they evolved to appeal to noctural insects and are so enticing that they need only a few hours each night to successfully pollenate.

Start a moon garden with plants from the list below. For an awe-inspiring effect, arrange the garden in the shape of a crescent or half moon.

NIGHTBLOOMERS

Jasmine tobacco

Moonflower

Night-blooming cereus cactus

Pink evening primrose

South African dimorphotheca

Toloachee

PLANTS THAT WILL COMPLEMENT YOUR MIDNIGHT GARDEN

African Iris (blooms resemble butterflies or fairies)

Artemisia (silver foliage)

Baby's breath (starry blooms glow under moonlight)

Dusty miller (silver foliage)

BUG-FREE COMFORT ZONE

Outdoor living means more neighbors—from fluttering butterflies and sparkling fireflies to biting mosquitoes, no-see-ums, and flies. Don't let the pests drive you back inside! Mosquitoes are hungriest at dawn and dusk, and the light of a full moon will bring out the bugs, but don't give up! Try these handy remedies for avoiding or repelling nuisances, without using toxic substances that might harm the helpful kinds of bugs.

FOR THE BODY

Wear light-colored clothes, since dark colors attract mosquitoes; wear shoes; stay dry—body moisture attracts bugs; apply a citrus or herb-based repellent. To make your own, boil 1 ounce (28 g) of green leaves from citriodora and chamomile plants in 1 gallon (3.8 L) of water. Strain and refrigerate the liquid. Splash it liberally on all exposed body parts before going outdoors.

FOR OUTDOOR SPACES

Light citronella candles and place them so that the smoke wafts your way—the smoke repels mosquitoes; keep an electric fan handy—it keeps air circulating and bugs at bay; plant a shoo-fly plant nearby; invest in lightbulbs that don't attract bugs, and install them in all outdoor fixtures.

IN THE YARD

Drain off standing water so there's no place for mosquitoes to breed; clean birdbaths weekly; eliminate tall grass and weeds, that are daytime mosquito habitats; plant natural repellents, such as chamomile, citriodora, and shoo-fly.

Moon & stars string o' lights

EVERY EVENING FEELS FESTIVE WITH THESE
NIGHT SKY-THEMED TWINKLE LIGHTS. DESIGNER
SKIP WADE ALSO SUGGESTS TWO ALTERNATIVES
TO ACCENT ANY PARTY OR DECORATIVE SCHEME.

DESIGNER:
SKIP WADE

INSTRUCTIONS
Preparing the cookie cutter frames

1 From the cutting edge of the cookie cutter, use metal snips to cut a square hole just large enough to thread a mini-light through. Center the hole in the side of the cutter.

2 Cut the vacuum cleaner belt into approximately ¾-inch (1.9 cm) pieces.

3 Cut a ½-inch (1.3 cm) "X" in the center of each belt section with the craft knife.

4 Attach the vacuum cleaner belt pieces with hot glue to the inside of the cookie cutter openings, centering the X in the opening you made.

Preparing the wax paper covers

1 Cut the wax paper into a 12 x 24-inch (30 x 61.5 cm) sheet.

2 Fold and crease the wax paper sheet in half, then open it out flat on a piece of craft paper. Over one half of the wax paper, shave the crayons with a hand-held pencil sharpener, scattering the shavings over the wax paper. Repeat with a second color.

3 Fold the clean half of the wax paper sheet over the half with the shavings, then cover it with two sheets of craft paper.

MATERIALS
Strand of small holiday lights

Cookie cutters, as many as needed for your string of lights

Rubber vacuum cleaner belt, ¾ inch (1.9 cm) wide

Wax paper

Craft paper

Wax crayons

TOOLS
Metal snips or very sharp scissors

Craft knife

Hot glue gun and glue sticks

Hand-held pencil sharpener

Iron

Felt-tip pen

4 With the iron set at a medium temperature (no steam), press the iron onto the sandwiched paper and shavings. Pull back the craft paper and check your progress after every second pass with the iron. Stop ironing when the crayon shavings have melted.

5 Let the wax paper cool for approximately five minutes.

6 Repeat with other pairs of color combinations, creating differently colored covers for each shape of cookie cutter (three different color combinations were used for the pictured lights).

Assembling the cookie cutter lights

1 Place the cookie cutters on top of the finished wax paper sheets; trace the cookie cutters onto the colored wax paper with a felt-tip pen, then flip the cookie cutter over and trace out the other side (each cookie cutter needs two covers).

2 Cut out the traced shapes with a craft knife.

3 Glue the edges of the cutout shapes to the cookie cutters with hot glue.

4 Insert a light into the openings that were cut in the cookie cutters.

VARIATIONS

Tiny flowerpot covers

MATERIALS

Strand of small holiday lights
Terra cotta pots, ½ inch (1.3 cm) in diameter
Silver spray paint
Sponge
Flat-head screwdriver
Hammer
Rubber bands

INSTRUCTIONS

1 Spray the insides of the pots with metallic silver paint, and allow them to dry. Place a flowerpot, upside down, on the sponge.

2 Use the screwdriver as a chisel and gently tap with the hammer to enlarge the small hole in the pot bottom so that the light will fit through it.

3 Insert the lights through each of the pots' holes, pulling the light through the hole and out of the pot. Wrap a rubber band around the light base to hold the light inside the pot.

Painted funnel covers

MATERIALS

Strand of small holiday lights
Small metal funnels, approximately 2½-inch (6.5 cm) diameter at the mouth
Red spray paint
Rubber bands

INSTRUCTIONS

1 Spray the outside of the funnels with red paint, and allow to dry.

2 Insert a light through the small end of each funnel.

3 Pull the light through the funnel end and out the mouth. Wrap a rubber band around the base of the light to keep it inside the funnel.

COLLECTOR'S PARADISE

Every collector appreciates the admiration of friends and family, but sometimes a particularly quirky medley will prompt alarming questions. "How many of those things do you need?" "What will you ever do with all that?" "Won't you just throw that out?" "Why are you doing this?"

If these questions sound familiar, don't give in to your critics; you've got the perfect place to show off your treasures—your porch or deck!

If old fans or toy trucks aren't welcome as household decorations, move them outside where you and your guests can admire them.

Gathered over many summers, seashells and transplanted river rocks alike will be happy for the exposure. The clay creations you, your children, grandchildren, nieces, or nephews made years ago don't have to be recognizable to anyone. Interesting is good, and all these items will serve as conversation starters with guests. Who knows, you might even start collecting things you never thought of before.

Lounging deck

Create the perfect barefoot lounging spot—a place where nothing much happens—with furniture that breaks the rules. Group the pieces to suit your needs and use the space in new ways; it's like having an outdoor family room. Now that you have the chance to catch up on some straw-hat summer reading, let your mind wander off to distant vistas. The delightful sound of a tiny trickling water fountain is the perfect accompaniment to your getaway afternoons on the deck.

Bubbling water garden

WATER PLANTS ARE SO EASY TO MAINTAIN, AND
SUSAN KIEFFER DESIGNED THIS WATER GARDEN
TO SOOTHE THE SOUL BY INCORPORATING A
TINY ADJUSTABLE FOUNTAIN.

DESIGNER:
SUSAN KIEFFER

MATERIALS

1-gallon (3.8 L) plastic milk
container

Terra-cotta planter bowl,
approximately 20 inches
(50 cm) in diameter

Silicone caulk

Water sealant

Spray paint (optional)

Semi-circular vinyl-coated wire
grid shelf unit, found at
home improvement centers

Potted bog plant, 4 inches
(10 cm) tall (available at
well-stocked garden centers)

Submersible pump

Bell fountainhead

River stones, polished river
rocks, and shells

Water plants (as available at
well-stocked garden centers)

TOOLS

Scissors

Plastic knife

Epoxy glue

Small plastic tub, for mixing
the epoxy

INSTRUCTIONS

1 Cut a flat 4-inch (10 cm) disk out
of the plastic carton. On the inside
of the terra-cotta planter, apply the
epoxy with the plastic knife to adhere
the edges of the disk to the pot and
cover the hole. Weight down the disk
until it is dry, approximately one hour.

2 Caulk the edges of the plastic disk.
Turn the planter over, and fill the
other side of the hole and its edges, in
about ½ inch (1.3 cm), with silicone
caulk. Let the caulk set 24 hours.

3 Spray the interior of the planter
with water sealant. Let it dry thoroughly. Apply a second coat and let it
dry. If desired, spray paint the exterior
of the planter.

4 Place the vinyl shelf into the
planter. Put the bog plant, still in
its nursery pot, in the bottom of the
planter. It may be necessary to cut ½
inch (1.3 cm) or so from the rim of the
plant container so that it will just fit
under the vinyl shelf. (Just be sure not
to cut below the soil line!) If you would
like the plant to sit higher in the
arrangement, place it on a small rock.

5 Remove the shelf and the bog
plant. Set the pump on its lowest
pressure setting (refer to the instructions with the pump) and place it
near the center of the planter, pressing down firmly so the suction cups
secure it to the bottom.

6 Set the vinyl shelf in the planter,
and position the bog plant at the
open end. Attach the bell fountain
spray head onto the pump through one
of the square holes in the vinyl grid.

7 Add water almost to the top of the rim of the bog plant, making sure that the pump's intake filters are covered.

8 Before plugging in the fountain, create a "drip loop" in the electrical cord. Make a small circle in the cord about 2 feet (60 cm) from the pump end, and loop the prongs through it. This will ensure that any water dripping down the cord will not drip into the electrical socket.

9 Arrange stones, rocks, and shells on the vinyl shelf, fully covering it. Arrange more water plants around the edges. Plug in the fountain, adjusting the bell spray nozzle until you get the sound you like. Make sure that the water does not splash over the edges.

10 Check the water level occasionally and add water if necessary, covering the intake filters by at least 1 inch (2.5 cm).

11 As a precaution, always remember to unplug your fountain before leaving the house.

12 An occasional cleaning, perhaps every three or four months, will maintain good pump performance, and rid all surfaces of algae and bacteria. Disassemble the fountain and wash the planter, stones, and vinyl shelf grid with warm soapy water. Rinse well. To clean the pump, brush with soapy water, and rinse well.

HOME REMEDIES FOR MILDEW

Because you can't control the humidity outdoors, it's a good idea to keep home remedies for mildew close at hand. Mildew is the growth of fungi or bacteria on wet natural and man-made objects. And mildew is stealthy. It can begin to grow wherever the relative humidity is more than 50 percent and the temperature above 60°F (15°C). It eats anything organic: from minuscule bits of cloth cushions to food crumbs. Shade and moisture are its allies.

Commercial products, such as paint and water sealants, are available with added mildewcides and fungicides, but they are toxic and must be handled with care, so why not try the natural route? The next time a black bloom of mildew threatens the finish and integrity of your side table or invites your deck to rot, try the following homegrown remedies to ward it off:

Mix bleach and water in a ratio of 1 part bleach to 16 parts water, and scrub the affected areas.

Regular sunning of linens, seat cushions, and rugs can help prevent mildew, if done on low–humidity days.

Two cups of brewed chamomile tea, cooled, is said to make a natural spray that safely repels mildew and fungus on plants.

Gilded bugs luminaria

PLACE SEVERAL OF THESE DELIGHTFULLY BUGGY LUMINARIA
ON THE PORCH STAIRS OR ALONG THE SIDES OF A PATHWAY
TO LIGHT THE WAY AT YOUR NEXT OUTDOOR PARTY.

DESIGNER:
JEAN TOMASO MOORE

MATERIALS
for 1 luminaria

8-inch (20 cm) diameter terra-cotta
    flowerpot

White acrylic craft paint

Gold spray paint

Several sheets of white tissue paper

Gold acrylic craft paint

Black rubber-stamp ink

Découpage medium

Spray acrylic sealer

Clean white sand

12-inch (30 cm) taper candles

Glass hurricane chimney,
    12 inches (30 cm) tall

TOOLS

Foam brush or sponge

Duct tape

Rubber stamps

Stamp pads

Scissors

INSTRUCTIONS

1 Sponge or brush slightly diluted white acrylic paint onto the outside of the flowerpot. Spray the insides of the pot with the gold paint.

2 From the inside, cover the bottom hole of the flowerpot with a small piece of duct tape.

3 Stamp pictures of bugs (the designer used grasshoppers, dragonflies, and bees on her pots) onto a sheet of tissue paper. Stamp approximately 20 images using the black ink and about 10 images using the gold acrylic paint.

4 When the images are dry, use scissors to cut away any excess tissue paper.

5 Brush the découpage medium onto each sheet of tissue paper and adhere it to the flowerpot in a pleasing, random pattern.

6 Once dry, spray on several coats of the clear acrylic sealer to protect your design from the elements.

7 Fill the pot with sand. Push the taper candle into the sand, then push in the glass chimney.

SUMMERTIME READS

A good book can make a mediocre day disappear and make a beautiful day glorious, so why not take advantage of the relaxing spaciousness of the great outdoors to get some reading done? Relax with a cool drink and a pillow, and luxuriate in a restful afternoon with these porchy classics:

She Stoops to Conquer OLIVER GOLDSMITH

Gone with the Wind MARGARET MITCHELL

Front Porch Tales PHILLIP GULLY

Cat on a Hot Tin Roof TENNESSEE WILLIAMS

A View from the Porch LUDLOW PORCH

"Flowerdy" table

DESIGNER TAMI BARRY USES A BRIGHT AND CASUAL
DRAWING STYLE TO SPICE UP AN ORDINARY SLATTED
TABLE; FIND ONE STRONG ENOUGH TO DO DOUBLE
DUTY AS A BENCH WHEN COMPANY DROPS BY.

DESIGNER:
TAMI BARRY

INSTRUCTIONS

1 Using the white primer and the 1½-inch (3.8 cm) brush, paint the table and let it dry.

2 Using the 1½ inch (3.8 cm) brush, paint the table with two coats of the teal paint, allowing the first coat to dry thoroughly before applying the second one.

3 Photocopy and enlarge the patterns for the daisies, leaves, and snakes (see figures 1, 2, and 3 on page 108). When the paint is dry, use the carbon paper to transfer the patterns to the table's top and legs. Use the photograph as a visual guide for placement.

4 Apply the daisy centers using the end of the 1-inch (2.5 cm) marker

dipped in purple and violet. Dip and swirl the marker in the paints between each application to slightly mix and blend the colors.

5 Using brilliant yellow-green and the ¾-inch (1.9 cm) brush, paint the insides of the outlines of the leaves.

6 Using the same brush dipped in green, paint wavy lines along the right side of each leaf. While the paint is still wet, dip the brush into brilliant yellow-green and trace back over the wavy lines. To produce a blended effect do not rinse the brush between strokes.

7 With the number 2 round brush and the cadmium yellow, paint the petals of the daisies.

MATERIALS

Sturdy table (the one in the photograph has 7 slats and measures 24 x 24 x 15 inches (62 x 62 x 37.5 cm)

White latex primer

Semi-gloss latex paint in teal green

Carbon transfer paper

Acrylic artists' colors in several shades of purple and violet, brilliant yellow-green, medium green, cadmium yellow, and black

Acrylic matte varnish

TOOLS

Paintbrush, 1½ inches (3.8 cm) wide

Felt-tip marker, 1 inch (2.5 cm) wide

Paintbrush, ¾ inch (1.9 cm) wide

Number 2 round paintbrush

Number 0 liner paintbrush

Paintbrush, ½ inch (1.3 cm) wide

Felt-tip marker, ½ inch (1.3 cm) wide

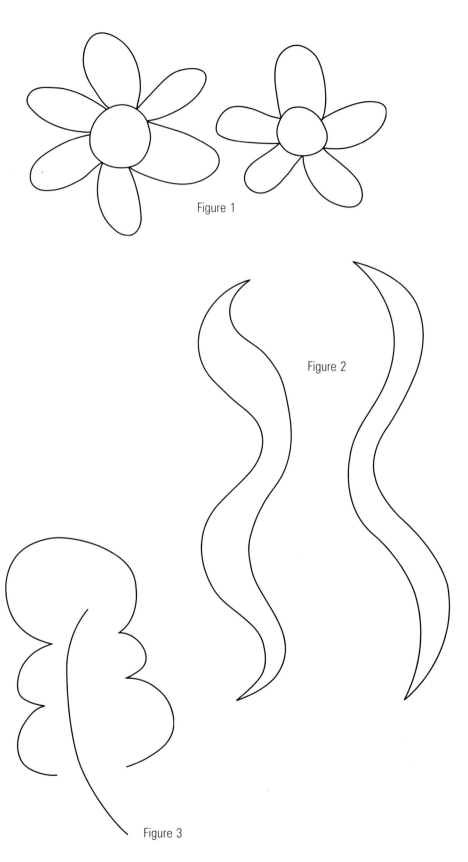

Figure 1

Figure 2

Figure 3

8 With black paint and the Number 0 liner brush, outline the petals and the centers of the daisies.

9 Dip the end of the paintbrush in violet, and use it to apply polka dots around the daisies.

10 Using a different violet paint, do the same around the leaves.

11 Use a deep violet and the ½-inch (1.3 cm) brush to paint inside the outlines of the snakes.

12 Dip the end of the ½-inch (1.3 cm) marker in cadmium yellow, and apply dots inside the curve of the snakes.

13 When the paint is dry, apply two coats of acrylic matte varnish. Allow the varnish to dry thoroughly between coats.

HOLDING IT DOWN

Paperwork doesn't feel like such a chore when it's done outdoors, but you need the right equipment.

Whether you escape the office for fresh air and a change of scenery, set up shop for the day, or catch up on your letter writing, the atmosphere is bound to relieve stress and fuel creativity.

The outdoor office does present a hazard: that breeze caressing your back can just as gently strew your papers aloft, shuffling them around the yard—or further. Chances are you aren't drinking from enough glasses to pin down all the piles and there aren't enough elbows available.

An assortment of paperweights is what you need to bear down on your work. Anything heavy and clean, that won't cut or stain your papers, will work.

Rustic trifold screen

THIS OPENWORK SCREEN LETS AIR AND LIGHT PASS THROUGH, AND HELPS CARVE A SMALLER SPACE OUT OF A LARGER ONE. IN THIS PROJECT, DESIGNER KEVIN BARNES USES WOOD FROM BRUSH PILES AND YARD TRIMMINGS TO CONSERVE NATURAL RESOURCES.

DESIGNER:
KEVIN BARNES

INSTRUCTIONS

1 Use wood from brush piles and yard trimmings. Remember, the length and size of the branches can be approximate measurements. Cut the branches with the pruning saw.

2 Build the three different sections of the screen. Each section uses four uprights and two crosspieces; lay them in position. Nail two crosspieces to the uprights, the first one 6 inches (15 cm) up from the bottom and the second one 6 inches (15 cm) down from the top. Use the longest nails possible without the point emerging from the other side of the branch.

3 Turn the three sections over.

4 Arrange the four filler branches in each of the panels, and nail them into place. Nail the two remaining crosspieces to the uprights, sandwiching in the filler branches.

5 Attach two leather hinges on either side of the middle screen, using two nails per hinge. The top and bottom hinges should be attached approximately 6 inches (15 cm) below the top and bottom crosspieces.

MATERIALS

6 branches, each measuring
   6½ feet (1.9 m) long and
   approximately 2 inches
   (5 cm) in diameter, for the
   uprights

12 branches, each measuring
   18 inches (45 cm), approximately 1 inch (2.5 cm) in
   diameter, for the crosspieces

12 lighter weight branches, at
   least 6½ feet (1.9 m) long,
   for filling in the panels

4 leather pieces, approximately
   2 x 12 inches (5 x 30 cm),
   for hinging the panels

Assorted sizes of nails

TOOLS

Pruning saw

Tape measure

Hammer

Bird-watcher's porch

The porch of this Georgian Revival is known as a true Queen Anne; it sports some Italianate and Neo-Classical touches, too. Typically, a large bay window is surrounded by an open porch that extends out from the covered veranda, lending itself to specialized seating areas for hobbies like bird-watching.

Quiet porch sitting has its own rewards when the yard is designed to attract native birds. Lure yellow finches and brilliant-throated hummingbirds with avarian delights, such as special feed and a birdbath. Keep the binoculars and a regional bird guide close at hand for the delightful moments when you spot your elusive quarry. With a little bit of patience, you'll soon be journaling your observations and comparing notes with Audubon.

MATERIALS

14 cedar wood shims, 1¼ inches (3.5 cm) wide, cut to 12-inch (30 cm) lengths, available at home improvement centers

2 craft wood disks, 6½ inches (16.3 cm) in diameter, or 2 rounds cut from plywood

1-inch (25 mm) brads

8-inch (20 cm) diameter plastic funnel

Approximately 300 miniature wood shingles, 1½ x ¾ inches (3.8 x 1.9 cm), found where dollhouse accessories are sold

Acrylic craft paint in leaf green, turquoise, and forest green

5 x 2-inch (12.5 x 5 cm) wooden finial

2 decorative wooden pegs with dowel ends, 1¼ inches (3.5 cm) long

18-gauge copper wire

Wooden bead, ¾ inch (1.9 cm) wide

3 or 4 glass beads

Miniature wood birdhouse, with a 2 x 2-inch (5 x 5 cm) base

Miniature gingerbread wood gable, 5 inches (12.5 cm) wide, found where dollhouse accessories are sold

Clear spray acrylic sealer

TOOLS

Scissors

Ruler

Duct tape

Small block of wood

Electric drill

Small bits and 1-inch (2.5 cm) paddle bit

Hammer

Utility knife

Strong adhesive

Paintbrush

Wood glue

Wire cutters

Pliers

Queen Anne's birdhouse

DESIGNER JEAN TOMASO MOORE MADE INGENIOUS USE OF DOLLHOUSE SUPPLIES TO CREATE A DECORATIVE BIRDHOUSE FIT FOR A QUEEN.

DESIGNER:
JEAN TOMASO MOORE

INSTRUCTIONS

1 Cut the shims to approximately 12 inches (30 cm) long, trimming them with the scissors at the thinner edge if necessary.

2 Line the shims up on a flat surface, making sure the bottom edges are lined up and even. Lay a strip of duct tape across the bottom and top sections of the shims. This holds the shims together so you can stand them up and nail them to the base.

3 Drape the shims over the small block of wood. Using the paddle bit, drill a 1-inch (2.5 cm) hole into the middle of a shim for the birdhouse entrance.

4 Place one of the wooden disks onto your work surface; this is the base of your birdhouse. Stand the row of shims upright and wrap them around the circular base until the two end pieces meet.

5 Drill a small pilot hole through a shim and into the base. Use a small brad to hold the shim in place. Do the same with all the shims, attaching each one to the base with a brad. When all the shims are attached, pull off the duct tape.

6 Place the second wooden disk into the top end of the birdhouse. Again, drill a pilot hole into each shim and hammer in the brads to hold all the pieces in place. When the shims are all nailed into place, lay the birdhouse on its side and nail another brad into each shim for added stability.

7 To make the birdhouse roof, cut the spout off the funnel, using a utility knife. Put a thick bead of adhesive along the outside bottom (wide end) of the funnel. Apply the shingles one at a time, overlapping and pressing each one down as you go; let the shingles overhang the funnel by ⅜ inch (9 mm). Start another layer of shingles about 1 inch (2.5 cm) above the first. Continue to layer the shingles until the roof is covered. Allow the adhesive to set for 24 hours.

8 Use a dilute wash of leaf green acrylic paint to color the body of the birdhouse. Paint the wooden finial and other wooden embellishments using combinations of green and turquoise paints.

9 Drill a small hole beneath the 1-inch (2.5 cm) birdhouse opening to accommodate the small painted wooden peg. Use a dab of wood glue to hold the peg in place. Drill a small hole into the end of the peg (to hold the copper wire). Fasten the ½-inch (1.9 cm) wooden bead to the end of the dowel with wood glue. Cut a 1½-inch (3.8 cm) piece of the copper wire, and thread a glass bead onto it. Use pliers to create a loop in the wire to hold the bead in place. Put a dab of adhesive onto the end of the wire and thread the wire through the wooden bead into the small hole in the dowel. This completes the perch.

10 Paint the roof shingles, using various combinations of the green paints. When the paint is dry, apply a thick bead of adhesive along the top perimeter of the house, and press the roof into place.

11 To assemble the rooftop decoration, first drill a hole into the top of the finial and also into the base of the miniature birdhouse; these holes will accommodate both ends of the small wooden peg. Use the wood glue to join the three pieces together (see figure 1). Also drill a small hole into the top of the miniature birdhouse roof, to hold a piece of copper wire.

12 Glue the entire assemblage together onto the peak of the roof, using a thick bead of adhesive.

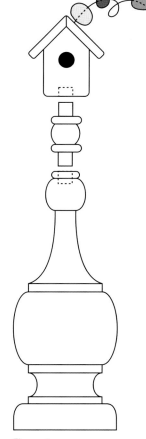

Figure 1

13 Fasten several glass beads onto a piece of copper wire approximately 3 inches (7.5 cm) long, and glue the wire into the small hole you drilled in the top of the miniature birdhouse.

14 Attach the gingerbread gable above the door of the house with wood glue. Tack a brad into the gable to help hold it in place.

15 When everything is in place and the glue is dry, use the clear acrylic sealer to protect the finish.

CAT'S CRADLE

This game of skill is played with string by two people. Popular the world over, it first came into use in the 19th century. It was originally called Cratch Cradle, because the design resembles a cratch, a storage bin for hay.

One player stretches a loop of yarn or string over the extended fingers of both hands. The second player removes the yarn without dropping the loops and tries to make another figure; try your skill!

Cottage style floorcloth

THE FLOOR OF YOUR PORCH OR DECK WILL BE BRIGHTENED BY THE SOFT, CASUAL DECORATIVE MOTIF ON THIS INEXPENSIVE COVERING. THIS FLOORCLOTH HAS A FIELD OF FLOWERS PRETTY ENOUGH TO ATTRACT HUMMINGBIRDS.

DESIGNER:
KATHY COOPER

MATERIALS

Piece of commercial-grade vinyl, approximately 4 x 6 feet (1.2 x 1.8 m)

Gesso or white latex house paint

Contact paper

Craft paint in light, medium, and dark green; white, beige, blue, and 2 colors of red

Thinning medium for paint

Acrylic varnish

Clear paste wax

TOOLS

Pruning shears or heavy scissors

Pencil

Nylon-bristle paintbrush, 3 inches (7.5 cm) wide

Paintbrush, 1½ inches (3.8 cm) wide

Soft, clean rags

Rubber comb, 4 inches (10 cm) wide

Aluminum pie plates or palette

Number 5 paintbrush

Sponge stamps in a leaf and a flower pattern

INSTRUCTIONS

Commercial-grade vinyl for floors comes in 6-foot (1.8 m) widths. Buy a remnant large enough for the project. Choose a vinyl with a low relief pattern, so that it will not be too prominent on the reverse side, where the painting will be done.

1 Lay out the vinyl in sunlight. Warming it makes it easier to cut.

2 With the pruning shears, cut the vinyl into a softly rounded rectangular shape.

3 With the pencil, mark out the design on the back side of the vinyl.

4 Use the 3-inch (7.5 cm) paintbrush to apply the base coat of gesso or the white latex house paint. Let the paint dry before doing each successive painting step.

5 Cut out squares and flower shapes from the contact paper. Peel off the backing paper and affix the squares to the perimeter. Arrange the flowers in a random pattern over the interior area.

6 Using the 1½-inch (3.8 cm) paintbrush, crosshatch the entire floorcloth with a glaze of thinned green craft paint. Use a 50/50 mixture to start, adjusting the transparency to suit your design.

7 With a damp rag, apply a darker green glaze by rolling the rag across the entire vinyl piece.

8 Repeat the rag-rolling method with a beige glaze.

9 Remove the contact paper stencils.

10 Paint the squares blue, then comb them with the 4-inch (10 cm) rubber comb in opposing directions.

11 To paint the irregularly shaped pink circles, put the two different reds and a white paint into separate pie plates, then dip the number 5 brush into each of them.

12 Paint the leaves freehand in a medium green, using the number 5 paintbrush.

13 Pour each of the green paints into the aluminum pie plates, and sponge-stamp the darker leaves onto the medium-green leaves, then stamp the lighter green leaves over those.

14 Stamp the blue flower shape in the center of each pink circle.

15 Swirl the yellow paint on top of each blue flower.

16 After the paint is dry, seal the entire floorcloth surface with acrylic varnish, using the 3-inch (7.5 cm) nylon-bristle brush. Apply at least two coats.

17 Wax with clear paste wax, applied with a soft clean rag. Let it air dry, then buff with the clean rag.

BUTTERFLY & BIRD GARDENS

You don't have to venture far to marvel at the butterfly's light, dancing movements, or enjoy a bird's songs and displays of ingenuity. Getting close to these fascinating, joy-inspiring creatures is easy—not to mention mutually beneficial—but it's up to us to provide safe havens. Both species require four elements: water, food, shelter, and places to raise their young. For their safety, don't use toxic pesticides around your home, and keep pets away.   In return for sanctuary, butterflies and birds will pollinate your flowers, eat insects by the hundreds, beautify your garden, and offer you hours of viewing pleasure—keep binoculars handy!

BUTTERFLIES

So long as rain and dew can puddle on foliage, butterflies will have plenty of moisture in most climates. They will also make use of puddles, birdbaths, and garden tubs.

Many butterflies feed on flower nectar, and most lay eggs on plants. Large patches of flowers are better than a scattered assortment. A garden with variety and abundance suits butterflies better than a rigid design. See the list below for plants that attract butterflies.

Butterflies must avoid wind and rain, which damage their wings. Provide protection with dense shrubs, trees, and fences. Butterflies also require daily doses of sunshine to warm their bodies. Rocks and sunny, cleared areas provide sunbathing opportunities.

BIRDS

Different birds need different food sources. Hummingbirds feed on nectar and prefer trumpet-shaped and red flowers. Finches, sparrows, and cardinals eat seed heads on faded flowers. Many birds gobble berries from bushes. Others feast on suet.

If you're feeding with bird seed, you'll have visitors year-round. Provide several squirrel-proof feeders to attract a greater variety of birds.

To keep your yard, porch, or deck clean, sweep or rake beneath the feeder regularly to remove fallen seed and droppings.

Clean feeders regularly in a bucket, using a solution of one part household chlorine bleach to nine parts water. This wards off bacteria that spreads disease among birds.

Not all birds will live in birdhouses, but most will take advantage of shrubs or trees with dense branching structures as nesting sites. Hedging and shearing discourages nesting. Dead trees also make good nest sites. Allowing your yard to have a natural, rather than manicured look will benefit the birds. Avoid disturbing nests—some birds will not return.

Birds need water to drink and bathe. Puddles will suffice. If you install birdbaths or garden tubs, make sure they have rough surfaces for sure footing. Clean and fill these water sources weekly.

Great Plants and Shrubs for Both Butterflies and Birds

Asters
Blue queen salvia
Butterfly plant
Coreopsis
Glossy abelia
Agarito

Plants and Shrubs for Butterflies

Asclepsia
Asters
Black-eyed Susans
Butterfly bush
Bee balm
Coreopsis
Cosmos
Honeysuckle
Joe-pye weed
Lavender
Lilacs
Milkweed
Nasturtiums
Pentas
Purple coneflowers
Zinnias

Shrubs and Bushes for Bird Nesting and Food

Juniper evergreens
Barberry
Holly
Laurel
Rhododendron

Photo by S. Tourtillott

Twig topiary form

DESIGNER MOLLY SIEBURG ADDED SOME
PIZZAZZ TO A PLANTER FILLED WITH IVY
BY CREATING A TOPIARY TWIG FORM BASED
ON A BIRD PROFILE. IF YOU DON'T HAVE
ACCESS TO THE NATURAL MATERIALS FOR
HARVESTING, THEY'RE READILY AVAILABLE
FROM A FLORIST OR CRAFT SUPPLY STORE.

DESIGNER:
MOLLY SIEBURG

INSTRUCTIONS

1 Cover the 12-inch (30 cm) lengths of florist wire with the brown floral tape. Twist a bit of tape onto the end of the wire and roll it diagonally down the wire, twisting and smoothing the tape with your fingers. Cover far more wire than you think you will need—30 pieces is a good start.

2 Make two bundles of your longest twigs with about six twigs in each bundle. Wire both ends of each bundle. Then, make an oval shape with the two bundles, securing the crossed ends with wire. This shape is the base of the bird's body.

3 Create two bundles as in step 2. Wire these bundles to the sides of the oval you created, to make a three-dimensional form.

4 Cut U-shaped pins about 5 inches (13 cm) long from the corners of wire coat hangers (you should be able to make eight pins with the four coat hangers). Use several pins to anchor the body base to the planted pot or planter.

5 Wire additional twigs to the sides of the body base as desired. Then, begin to fill the body base loosely with angel vine or Spanish moss. Twigs can be tucked in without wiring at this stage, to further define the shape.

6 Take six twigs in hand and bend them so that the ends overlap, to create a small oval shape for the head. Overlap the ends, then wire the shape about 4 to 6 inches (10 to 15 cm) in from the ends, to create a beak.

7 Make the head shape more three-dimensional, as you did in step 3. When you are satisfied with the shape, wire it to the body.

8 Fill the head shape loosely with angel vine. Add additional twigs to the head shape if needed.

9 To create a tail, wire a handful of twigs at the base. Make two additional bunches. Push a bundle of twigs into the soil at the back of the bird body. Place the other two bundles on each side. Add additional twigs to make the tail fuller.

10 Twine some of the planted ivy on the bird form. Add a ribbon around the neck if you like. For special occasions, decorate the form with cut flowers.

MATERIALS

12-inch (30 cm) lengths of florist wire

Brown floral tape

Birch, willow or other supple young twigs (if you use twigs, soak them in a bucket of water overnight to make them more supple)

4 wire coat hangers

Large terra-cotta pot or planter filled with soil and planted with vines

Angel vine (available in dried floral supply section of craft stores) or substitute Spanish moss, wood excelsior, or honeysuckle vines for filling in the figure

TOOLS

Heavy duty scissors or garden shears

Wire cutters

Patinaed *birdbath table*

METAL GARDEN ORNAMENTS WITH FINE LAYERS OF PATINA ARE EXPENSIVE AND HARD TO FIND. DESIGNER TERRY TAYLOR SIMULATED THE LOOK WHEN HE TRANSFORMED A CONCRETE BIRDBATH INTO A DISTINCTIVE TABLE.

DESIGNER:
TERRY TAYLOR

MATERIALS

Concrete birdbath stand and top

Acrylic latex primer (any color)

Matte or satin latex enamel paint (black or brown)

Commercial patina paint containing iron filings (sold as a rust finish)

Commercial antiquing solution containing ammonium chloride and copper sulfate

Matte acrylic sealer

Glass tabletop (sized to fit your birdbath top)

Glass marbles

TOOLS

Rasp, file, or abrasive pads

Garden hose

Disposable brushes

Containers for the paints and patina solution

Look for bargains on concrete garden ornaments by visiting out-of-the-way garden shops that very often sell seconds that have more air bubbles in the surface of the ornament. Large garden centers will usually discount chipped ornaments that may suit your purpose. The range of commercial patina paints is impressive. Rust, verdigris, antique blue, gold, copper, and silver are readily available in craft and paint stores.

INSTRUCTIONS

1 If your birdbath base has any seam imperfections, use a file or abrasive pad to smooth out the seams.

2 Make sure that the concrete base is free of dust and dirt. Wash it with a garden hose and allow it to dry thoroughly before using the patina materials.

3 Seal the concrete birdbath with a coat of the acrylic primer. Use whatever primer you may have on hand from other home decorating projects—color is not important. Allow the primer to dry thoroughly.

4 Paint the birdbath with a coat of the acrylic paint. If you are creating a rust patina, use black or brown as an undercoat. Allow this coat of paint to dry.

5 Use a disposable brush and follow the manufacturer's instructions for applying the patina paint; two or three coats will be sufficient.

6 Allow the final coat of patina paint to dry for 12 hours or more, then use a disposable brush to apply a coat of the antiquing solution. Allow it to dry. Reapply additional coats as needed until you have the patina look you want.

7 Give the birdbath base a light coat of the matte acrylic sealer. Be sure you apply a very light coat, as the sealer can change the look of the patina. Allow it to dry, then give it a second light coat.

8 Fill the bowl with the glass marbles, then set the glass tabletop on the birdbath.

Designers

KEVIN BARNES builds rustic indoor and outdoor furniture and art pieces. He is also the creator of outdoor sanctuary spaces.

LOVEETA BAKER is a designer living in Asheville, North Carolina.

TAMI BARRY is a professonal functional-art designer whose whimsical line of furniture, shoes, and glassware can be found throughout Western North Carolina. Her studio is located at 166 West Haywood St #3, Asheville, North Carolina 28801. (828) 232-1177

KATHY COOPER is an expert designer, artist, and author of *The Complete Book of Floorcloths* and *Weekend Crafter Series: Painting Floorcloths* (Lark Books). Visit Kathy's website at www.Kathycooperfloorcloths.com

SUSAN KINNEY (B.F.A. in Sculpture/ Ceramics and B. A. in Art History) is a designer who specializes in eclectic interiors, glass and clay jewelry, fabric and rug design, and computer-generated artwork of all kinds.

ROLF HOLMQUIST is an artist and print-maker who lives in the cabin he built in Burnsville, North Carolina.

AMY JOHNSON is a native of North Carolina. She has worked with clay for the last ten years at her Iron Duff Studio near Waynesville, North Carolina.

SUSAN KIEFFER has enjoyed dabbling in crafts all of her life. She lived in the Florida Keys for many years, but traded the sea for the mountains of Asheville, North Carolina, where she currently works for the Folkwear Pattern division of Lark Books. Check out more of her fountains in *Tabletop Fountains* (Lark Books).

JEAN TOMASO MOORE, a part-time multi-media artist, has been creating art in one form or another for as long as she can remember. She lives with her humble and patient husband in the beautiful hills of Asheville, North Carolina. Contact Jean at www.LeaningTowerArt@aol.com.

MOLLY SIEBURG has a background in painting and floral design. She currently uses her talents at the Gardener's Cottage, a flower/garden/antique store in Asheville, North Carolina, where she is part-owner and responsible for most of the buying and all of the displays.

TERRY TAYLOR'S interest du jour is working with sterling silver and other metals in jewelry. He is a prolific designer and exhibiting artist, who lives in Asheville, North Carolina.

DERICK TICKLE teaches Decorative Painting and Restoration in Asheville, NC. Trained in England as an apprentice, he is an examiner and advisor for the City and Guilds of London in Decorative Painting. He has run workshops and seminars for TV set designers, interior decorators, and

professionals in Britain, New Zealand, and America. His e-mail address is DTickle2@aol.com.

SUSAN KINNEY is a designer specializing in eclectic interiors, glass and clay jewelry, fabric and rug design, and computer generated artwork. She has degrees in Sculpture/Ceramics and Art History and over 25 years of experience in various design fields, including raku pottery and one of a kind wearable art. Susan attributes some of her ideas to the oriental influences experienced while living in Hawaii and Japan. Her e-mail address is SuezenDesigns@home.com

TRAVIS WALDREN is a semi-retired feminist psychotherapist who now runs her own fiber art and textile design studio, Wicked by Nature©. She resides with her two dogs and visiting strays in the mountains outside Asheville, North Carolina.

CATHY SMITH works in a variety of media. She is currently following her destiny in western North Carolina, accompanied and encouraged in this pursuit by husband, son, and assorted feline, canine, and reptilian family members.

MICHAEL SAARI studied ornamental metalwork in Europe, and holds an M.F.A. in sculpture. A master blacksmith, he is known for his workshops and commissions in both historic and contemporary forged metal. Contact him at Michael J. Saari Workshop & Studio, 256 Childs Hill Road, Woodstock, CT 06281 (860)928-0257

Index